INSIDE THE SUSTAINABLE DEVELOPMENT GOALS

The Sustainable Development Goals (SDGs) came with bold promises: ending poverty, saving the planet, and making this world a better place by 2030. But being in the second halftime, there is too little progress and too many setbacks. Drawing on the expertise of an author who has been actively involved in negotiating and later implementing the SDGs, this book offers a unique insider view into the behind-the-scenes processes. It relates the SDGs and their aims of fighting poverty and achieving sustainability to the bigger picture of politics, economics, and vested interests, breaking down dependencies and alliances, expectations and motives. It uncovers and dissects the politics and interests that shaped the SDGs from the very beginning, as well as the drivers behind propelling or curtailing sustainable development.

This book is an indispensable and comprehensive guide to the SDGs. It outlines where they came from, how they are being implemented, the main lessons learned so far, and what to conclude for the years ahead. As the deadline of 2030 is close, and discussions about what should come after the SDGs are imminent, this book is among the first to draw conclusions for the post-2030 era, what to expect, and what to demand from a potential successor agenda.

This book addresses policymakers, practitioners, researchers, and students alike, as well as anyone interested in poverty, environment, and sustainability. Written in a highly accessible style, this book also breaks down the United Nations and its processes and institutions, how they are enabling but also limiting the SDGs and the sustainability agenda in general.

Adele Orosz has held various senior positions with the German Federal Foreign Office, the German Federal Ministry for Economic Cooperation and Development, in particular as a Senior Advisor to the State Secretary, the United Nations Development Programme (UNDP) in

New York and the European External Action Service (EEAS) in Brussels. She was a member of the EU negotiation team on the 2030 Agenda for Sustainable Development, adopted in 2015. The subsequent years, she worked on implementing the SDGs in different roles. She has a long track record in international affairs and development cooperation, and has worked extensively on governance, conflict, and crisis, in particular in the Sahel and the Middle East, as well as sustainable development. Before working in international relations and development, she was a journalist. She holds a PhD and two Master's degrees in International Relations, Political Science, and Journalism.

Routledge Studies in Sustainable Development

This series uniquely brings together original and cutting-edge research on sustainable development. The books in this series tackle difficult and important issues in sustainable development including: values and ethics; sustainability in higher education; climate compatible development; resilience; capitalism and de-growth; sustainable urban development; gender and participation; and well-being.

Drawing on a wide range of disciplines, the series promotes interdisciplinary research for an international readership. The series was recommended in the *Guardian*'s suggested reads on development and the environment.

Implementing Sustainable Cities
Edited by Sylvie Albert, Jeremy Millard, and Manish Pandey

Sustainable Urban Development in the European Arctic
Dorothea Wehrmann, Michał Łuszczuk, Katarzyna Radzik-Maruszak, Jacqueline Götze, and Arne Riedel

A Nordic Smart Sustainable City
Lessons from Theory and Practice
Barbara Maria Sageidet, Daniela Müller-Eie, and Kristiane M.F. Lindland

Inside the Sustainable Development Goals
From Fighting Poverty to Saving the World
Adele Orosz

For more information about this series, please visit: www.routledge.com/Routledge-Studies-in-Sustainable-Development/book-series/RSSD

INSIDE THE SUSTAINABLE DEVELOPMENT GOALS

From Fighting Poverty to Saving the World

Adele Orosz

Routledge
Taylor & Francis Group
LONDON AND NEW YORK

earthscan
from Routledge

Designed cover image: Shutterstock

First published 2025
by Routledge
4 Park Square, Milton Park, Abingdon, Oxon OX14 4RN

and by Routledge
605 Third Avenue, New York, NY 10158

Routledge is an imprint of the Taylor & Francis Group, an informa business

British Library Cataloguing-in-Publication Data
A catalogue record for this book is available from the British Library

ISBN: 9781032702643 (hbk)
ISBN: 9781032702612 (pbk)
ISBN: 9781032702681 (ebk)

DOI: 10.4324/9781032702681

Typeset in Sabon
by codeMantra

The views, thoughts, and opinions expressed in this book reflect solely those of the author, and not necessarily those of any current or previous employer.

CONTENTS

FOREWORD

The Sustainable Development Goals are a uniquely ambitious and comprehensive blueprint for the development of humanity and preservation of our planet. Negotiated and agreed in 2015 by all 193 UN member states, the Goals aim to "transform the world" by 2030. In the SDGs, and the wider 2030 Agenda for Sustainable Development to which they belong, the world has come up with a single universal framework for sustainable development which spans the latter's three dimensions (the economic, the social, and the environmental). Every Government has committed itself to implementing the 17 Goals and 169 targets, or sub-goals, by 2030. And many other stakeholders, from the private sector to civil society and the scientific and academic communities, have made the same commitment.

Not long after the halfway-point to 2030, how is the world faring? How likely are we to realize the ambitions we set for ourselves in 2015? We have had to deal with several major shocks on the way which could not easily have been foreseen: with a global pandemic and with the fall-out from Russia's invasion of Ukraine, to name but two. Measured in terms of progress so far on the individual targets, the picture is not encouraging. But, if we look at the political and public support which the SDGs continue to enjoy around the world, there is reason to be more hopeful.

In this incisive, thought-provoking, and well-researched study, Adele Orosz asks a number of searching questions about the SDGs. She looks at some of the shortcomings which have become apparent after nine years of implementation – or which, indeed, many have been present from the outset. She assesses the challenges of an integrated agenda where transformative progress can often depend not merely on achieving individual Goals and targets but on recognizing, and acting on, the multiple interconnections between them. Is the "complexity" of the SDGs an inevitability if policy coherence is to remain fundamental to development effectiveness? Or do we risk over-burdening Governments with this and adding also to the considerable challenges around public communication of the SDGs?

These are among many questions and dilemmas which are skillfully dissected by the author. These include the challenge of generating data worldwide for the measurement of progress; the urgent need to expand access to finance for achieving the SDGs; and the critical role which must be played by the private sector if the promise of the SDGs is to be fulfilled. Adele Orosz also gives a vivid account of the 2014–2015 negotiations which led to their adoption and looks ahead to the successor agenda which will be needed after 2030.

This is a timely and accessible book which takes the reader in detail through the evolution of the SDGs, their strengths and weaknesses, and their prospects for achievement in the medium to longer term. It will make an important contribution to the international debate on this subject.

David Donoghue
Former Irish Ambassador to the UN, co-facilitator of the 2014–2015 negotiations on the 2030 Agenda

ACKNOWLEDGMENTS

This is the place where I want to express my deep and sincere gratitude to the many friends, colleagues, professionals, and experts that provided their invaluable and profound insights and feedback, took the time for being interviewed and/or reading the progressing versions of the manuscript. I wish to express my special thanks to Marianne Beisheim (German Institute for International and Security Affairs), Claire Bonnel (Siemens Healthineers), Joe Colombano (Office of the UN Resident Coordinator to China), Stefanos Fotiou (FAO), Gerbrand Haverkamp (World Benchmarking Alliance), John Hendra (former UN Assistant Secretary-General, JD Hendra Strategic Consulting), Oli Henman (Action for Sustainable Development), Lisa Kurbiel (Joint SDG Fund), Michael McManus (IOM), Mitsuaki Mizuno (Ministry of Foreign Affairs of Japan), Ozonnia Ojielo (UN Resident Coordinator and Representative of the UN Secretary-General in Ruanda), Sabina Woelkner (Konrad-Adenauer Foundation), Elizabeth Maruma (UNEP), Sameh Al-Muqdadi (Green Charter GC, Germany), Omar Al-Ubaydli (Bahrain Center for Strategic, International and Energy Studies), and Bourhan Yassin (Rainforest Connection).

Since there is nothing more insightful and inspiring than discussing the SDGs and sustainable development with students who want to change the world, I am very grateful for the discussions I had with Sameh Al-Muqdadi and his students who relentlessly put into question many facets of conventional wisdom and keep on searching for how to really turn this world into a more sustainable place: Ahmed Alaa Mouhsen, Ahmed Hasim Saadoon, Basma Al-Kinani, Dunya Al-Hayali, Sama Yas, Nechirvan Kalary, Zahraa Obaid, Mariam Muhanned Majid, and Nasr Alani. I am wishing them all the best for whatever lies ahead and, most of all, to never give up fighting for a better world.

I particularly want to thank David Donoghue, former Irish Ambassador to the UN, co-facilitator of the 2014–2015 negotiations on the

2030 Agenda. He not only wrote the foreword to this book, but most of all was a great conversation partner and a true source of inspiration. We both had the privilege that we were part of the SDGs since the very beginning, he as Irish Ambassador to the UN and me as a member of the EU post-2015 negotiation team in Brussels, responsible for Goal 16. I very much enjoyed looking back at the post-2015 negotiation process, where I first met David, and all the highs and lows we went through during those tumultuous years. We are both still passionate about and working for the SDGs; therefore, it was even more exciting to reconnect with him and discuss this book project. Pondering about the flowers and fruits that have grown out of the SDGs since then, but also acknowledging where we had hoped for more and where the world needs to do better was an important part of our conversations. They have helped me a lot in putting my opinions and views into perspective and in hopefully producing some valuable insights and guidance about the SDGs and the journey of going sustainable. Writing this book was an incredibly profound experience, where I eventually felt it was extremely important to see the bigger picture, not only about the SDGs but the sustainability journey in general. In addition, my postings in New York, Berlin, and Baghdad during the past years offered important opportunities to see and reflect how the SDGs can make a difference and what it takes to go sustainable.

Finally, I am extremely grateful to my husband Christian who is my unwavering support throughout life and everything I do.

ABBREVIATIONS

CBD	Convention on Biological Diversity
COP	Conference of the Parties
DAC	Development Assistance Committee
FAO	Food and Agriculture Organization of the United Nations
FDI	Foreign Direct Investments
FfD	Financing for Development
GDP	Gross Domestic Product
GNI	Gross National Income
HLPF	High-Level Political Forum
IBRD	International Bank for Reconstruction and Development
IDGs	International Development Goals
IEA	International Energy Agency
IMF	International Monetary Fund
IOM	International Organization for Migration
IPCC	Intergovernmental Panel on Climate Change
IRENA	International Renewable Energy Agency
LDC	Least-Developed Country
LIC	Low-Income Country
MDGs	Millennium Development Goals
MIC	Middle-Income Country
NGO	Non-Governmental Organization
ODA	Official Development Assistance
OECD	Organization for Economic Cooperation and Development
OWG	Open Working Group
PPP	Purchasing Power Parity
SDGs	Sustainable Development Goals
SIDS	Small Island Developing States
UNDESA	United Nations Department of Economic and Social Affairs
UNDP	United Nations Development Programme
UNEP	United Nations Environmental Programme

UNFCCC	United Nations Framework Convention on Climate Change
UNODC	United Nations Office on Drugs and Crime
UNSD	United Nations Statistics Division
VNR	Voluntary National Review
WHO	World Health Organization

1

INTRODUCTION

The Sustainable Development Goals (SDGs) came with bold promises: ending poverty and saving the planet by setting out together on the path toward sustainable development until 2030. When the 2030 Agenda for Sustainable Development was adopted in September 2015 at the United Nations, the big grandeur accompanying this event was overwhelming, imbued in historic comparisons, denoting the agenda as a landmark of progress of human civilization, showcasing its resolve to make this world a better place. Most of those who participated in the negotiations in the beginning hardly believed something like this would ever be possible. Despite being the result of a hodgepodge of politics, power play, competition over attention and resources, heated debates with civil society, science and vested interests, and controversies over ethics and values, the 2030 Agenda is, indeed, a surprisingly ambitious and comprehensive agreement. In fact, this agenda with its 17 SDGs is one of the most complex and challenging endeavors ever decided in the framework of the United Nations.

But the big fanfare of UN member states agreeing on the SDGs and bringing them into this world has long faded. The world is in the thick of implementing them, with a mid-term balance that is extremely worrying and bleak with too little progress and too many setbacks. In the second half of their implementation time, the SDGs promise for a better future and decent, peaceful, and sustainable life on earth is in such deep trouble that the UN Secretary-General in 2023 called for a rescue plan for the SDGs, warning "the 2030 Agenda could become an epitaph for a world that might have been" (United Nations 2023: 2). Very soberingly and disappointingly, most steps toward advancing sustainability seem too little, too late, and there is even development in reverse happening. The world is witnessing stagnating progress in the fight against poverty, increasing violence and conflicts with record numbers of refugees and displaced people, continued polluting, draining, and overstretching of

DOI: 10.4324/9781032702681-1

natural ecosystems, and mounting environmental degradation with no shortage of looming doomsday scenarios.

However, going sustainable is not an option, but it is imperative for a healthy planet which is the indispensable basis for a decent, peaceful future for human life on earth. The little progress on the SDGs, combined with multiple crises and projections of existential threats humankind will undeniably be facing with business as usual, instantly provokes the question why the sustainability journey is facing so many difficulties. There are potentially many explanations that need to be explored further: key actors could be lacking the capacities or the political will to heed the call, the 2030 Agenda could not be providing the necessary guidance for going sustainable, being too weak, too lofty on key elements or missing some of them out completely, or the 2030 Agenda could have lost its in 2015 celebrated purpose and role as a guiding light showing the way for going sustainable.

Preceding the adoption of the SDGs were more than three years passionately and controversially debating, arguing, and churning through what a better future for all humankind and the planet should look like. Being the product of merging the poverty and environmental agenda and adding the economic dimension, the SDGs pursue in fact two overarching aims: one is eradicating poverty for good, and the other is transforming all human activities on earth to make them respect planetary boundaries. As noble and aspirational these aims sound, as difficult they are to achieve in real life. Regarding fighting poverty, there are no easy-to-replicate success formulas, and in some places, poverty is deeply entrenched and trapped in repeating cycles of conflict and crisis. Regarding transforming all human activities, poor countries, inclined to prioritize growth over protecting the environment, are anxious to catch up and reach prosperity and wellbeing, and rich countries, reluctant to give up convenient and comfortable lifestyles, are afraid to lose prosperity and wellbeing. And despite impressing advances in research and innovation, in many realms of human activity, truly sustainable living and working patterns, respecting planetary boundaries still need to be developed. While eradicating poverty was largely uncontested and supposed to produce winners only, going sustainable, however, is much more controversial, supposed to produce both winners and losers. Thus, heated debates about what going sustainable in daily life means, about the right policies and approaches, and about the right pace and scale, are ubiquitous. Identifying and implementing truly sustainable solutions for living and working easily triggers disagreement, denial, and backlashes in politics, economics, and societies all over the world, making this sustainability journey an extremely difficult endeavor.

But the science is very clear about the urgent need to go sustainable and to fundamentally change current lifestyles. Hence, it is essential to understand the strengths and weaknesses of the 2030 Agenda and what it can do for the world. Despite all disappointment and setbacks, as of now, the SDGs are the best shot available and the only global plan how to work for a more sustainable tomorrow for everyone and everywhere. Thus, being in the second halftime of the SDG era, this book aims at analyzing what they have been able to deliver so far and where they clearly have fallen short of their self-proclaimed promise to be a game-changer. It aims at outlining where and why key actors are getting engaged or are dragging their feet and what this means for the thorough transformation towards sustainability, as promised in the 2030 Agenda to happen all over the world. There is no doubt that a continued overstepping of planetary boundaries would have such devastating and irreversible impacts that it is indispensable to propel rethinking, remodeling, and remaking human life on earth. The SDGs, undoubtedly, have a role in this, but what exactly this looks like is a developing story.

With the 2030 deadline looming, there is, of course, the obvious question about the chances of achieving the SDGs by 2030: if UN member countries will be able to fulfill the pledges made in September 2015. Worryingly, the picture is very sobering, with deeply troubling setbacks, even reversals of development gains. The COVID-19 pandemic and the wars in Ukraine and the Middle East alone have heavily contributed to derailing many development paths. It doesn't take a fortune teller to make the insipid prediction that there is much potential for missing many SDGs by 2030 and for many people still not living happy decent lives. Sadly, there are projections saying that at current pace even achieving the SDGs by 2050 looks unlikely. Hence, it is essential to analyze the impact of the SDGs in the different policy fields: why there is progress in some areas, while other SDGs are lagging far behind. Another question of a more fundamental and principal nature is, if the SDGs are providing the needed guidance for making the world sustainable, and if fulfilling all of them would turn the world into a truly sustainable, peaceful, and happy place. Going sustainable is a popular buzzword, but also full of underestimated complexity and controversy, woefully lacking simple solutions and easily provoking backlashes. Hence, it is key to understand what going sustainable means and where the particular challenges and open questions are, as well as potential pitfalls or side effects. Thus, this book will scrutinize the goals and targets and if they set the right marks to be reached and enable countries, societies, and economies to achieve them, including the financial and other means needed to take action.

Finally, there is the question about the lessons learned so far and the takeaways from several years living in the SDG era. For the time remaining until 2030, it is imperative to discuss options regarding how to accelerate progress on the SDGs, where possible, and how to best make use of the remaining years. For the time after 2030, it is essential to look into the legacy of the SDGs, what to feed from the SDG experience into the post-2030 era. Now is the time to start debating options and inputs into a successor agenda, what to expect and demand from the post-2030 era, and how to enable the world to tackle the pressing sustainability challenges of this century.

When analyzing the SDGs and their role in setting the world out on the path toward sustainable development, it is important to understand which ideas shaped the term sustainability in the first place and how it materialized in an agenda at the United Nations. Therefore, Chapter 2 will be exploring the origins of the concept of sustainability. It will be tracing how depletion and pollution, decisively accelerating during the Industrial Revolution, already centuries ago triggered initial discussions about going sustainable. This once supposed luxury was set to morph into a question of survival many years later. In particular in the 1970s and 1980s, some deep cracks started emerging in the dream of wellbeing and continued economic growth of the developed world, tarnishing the so-far shining prosperity model. Evidence was piling up that the industrialized countries were terribly overstretching planetary boundaries and causing long-lasting environmental damage. Concurrently, millions of people were still mired in poverty and destitution and anxious to emulate and reach exactly that same unsustainable overshoot model. Obviously, the economic example set by the rich countries that was seen as a success formula for prosperity and wellbeing was leading the whole world onto a dangerous path of irreversibly changing and damaging the environment in a way that could be self-destructive for humankind.

The Stockholm Environment Conference in 1972 was a first major milestone and a turning point in bringing the world together over the rising challenges emanating from the harmful human impact on the earth's ecosystems. This chapter will explore how this event, in fact, laid the foundations for the global environmental agenda about sustainability, though without leading to specific further action at the time. But environmental damage through human action was becoming more palpable and severe, and growth and development somehow had to be reconciled with their impacts on nature and environment on a global level. Hence, the environmental agenda took roots at the United Nations which usually is the place to go for tackling global challenges. However, it took many alarming reports until the world eventually would come together in the so-called Earth summits: Rio in 1992 and Rio+20 in 2012. One major bone of contention for many years had been, if traditional economic growth still was the golden path out of poverty that just needed to be adapted to some environmental requirements, while postponing the most severe environmental questions to sometime later. Or, if potentially radical and fundamental changes in all economic systems and prosperity models all over the world were needed, as the environmental side effects of traditional growth were too severe and long-lasting and didn't allow to be delayed. Disappointingly, both Rio summits, although unprecedented in scope and scale, didn't manage to set up an all-encompassing environmental agenda. Apart from some few, though rather progressive decisions on single issues, like setting up the climate agenda, the outcome wasn't powerful enough for decisive action toward sustainability. Nevertheless, amid all disappointment, the delegations in Rio 2012 miraculously managed to at least agree on how to move on with the sustainability agenda, how to potentially renew and revitalize global efforts and give it a fresh start.

In the meantime, the poverty agenda had made its own way through the United Nations. After decades of ideologically charged debates about colonial legacies and burdens, responsibility and compensation, with the end of the Cold War, the development community managed to turn to a more pragmatic way of tackling this scourge of humanity. Fighting poverty was increasingly understood as a win–win for all countries, as obviously the whole world would benefit from more prosperity, trade, peaceful living together, and thriving economies. Thus, taking action to eliminate poverty at scale became a growing policy field. Driven by this win–win narrative, the poverty agenda was clearly a lot less controversial than the environmental agenda and was widely embraced and appreciated.

Thus, this chapter will look into the intensified discussions, in particular at the UN, about a new global poverty agenda, that eventually ushered in the Millennium Declaration and the Millennium Development Goals (MDGs). Running from 2000 to 2015, it was the first comprehensive global plan to eradicate poverty on earth. At the time, the world was broadly divided into two categories of countries: those that had reached unprecedented and enviable levels of wellbeing and prosperity, and those that were hoping and struggling to sooner or later be able to catch up and reach an equivalent level of wellbeing. The MDGs, basically, aimed at supporting the developing countries in eliminating the worst destitutions to enable them to eventually reach the same prosperity level as the developed countries. In a nutshell, the rich countries, the model to follow and emulate, should assist the poor countries, in the long run, to become one of them.

During the MDG era until 2015, the world witnessed tremendous development successes. And yet after 15 years, the fight against poverty was far from over; hence, it was undisputed that there should be some kind of successor agreement. Concurrently, the rise of the middle-income countries had bleakly laid bare like under a magnifying glass the often-overlooked downside of many development successes. There was no denying that there was a terrifying environmental price tag that came with development based on traditional growth. Lifting millions out of poverty and turning them into middle-class consumers meant millions more contributing to a heavy environmental footprint. The prevailing supposed success model for a good life came with devastating environmental repercussions at scale. Subsequently, the buzzword sustainability entered the development scene and was shedding a new light on food systems, trade, transport, energy, mobility, housing, and finance or fiscal regulation. While there was undisputed agreement that the fight against poverty had to continue, there was a growing fear about the repercussions of that fight. Or simply put, there was an eerie conundrum that if the entire global population enjoyed growth and prosperity like in the rich countries, nature and the earth's ecosystems would be brought to the brink of collapse. In the 1970s, this had been a rather theoretical projection and academic discussion, but now this prophecy was on its self-fulfilling path. The planetary limits of what the earth could sustain had become tangible, visible, breathable, and most importantly, measurable as well as predictable.

The fundamental question was how all people on earth, the present and the future generations, could possibly lead decent lives without pushing humankind and earth into some kind of doomsday scenario. This chapter will outline that the Rio track would have been the right place for identifying answers to this question but, with some exceptions, had largely ended up disappointing the high-flying expectations about providing guidance for a new global environmental agenda. Nevertheless, rather unexpectedly, the Rio+20 summit in 2012 eventually took the bold decision to merge the environmental and the poverty agenda as both were obviously and inexorably interlinked and intertwined. The aim was to produce a new and comprehensive global agenda for the world, and make the joint case for globally reaching sustainability. Thus, this chapter will be analyzing how the foundations were laid for the subsequent post-2015 process, named after the expiration of the MDGs that year, and how this shaped the ensuing negotiations. Although most UN member states in the beginning were rather unsure about the possible specific outcome of this post-2015 process, in hindsight it would be regarded as the dawning of a new era, the one of the Sustainable Development Goals (SDGs)

The analysis of Chapter 3 will be about the bumpy road that led to the SDGs, the post-2015 process, the drafting and negotiating in the framework of the United Nations. It will explore which expectations and doubts were floating around, which desires and constraints emerged that needed to be incorporated, and who and what shaped the outcome. The journey to the SDGs was remarkable in many ways. Preceding was a vast and comprehensive outreach and consultation process to set the scene for the negotiations: the High-Level Panel of Eminent Persons and the UN platform "The World We Want," in fact, asked everyone to weigh in and make all voices heard. The subsequent Open-Working Group (OWG) at the UN, tasked to prepare the official negotiations and draft a set of SDGs, provided a unique opportunity for all delegations involved to learn and understand what sustainability really was about. A so-called stocktaking phase aimed at fostering a sound thorough understanding of the interlinkages between poverty and the environment, between poor people turning into middle-class consumers and the subsequent ecological footprint, between enhancing agricultural output and harming biodiversity, or the impact of inequality, gender, good governance, and effective institutions on development.

It should not be underestimated that the post-2015 process was aiming at merging two worlds that had been existing apart for decades: the poverty agenda and the environmental agenda. These two agendas, with different mindsets and systems, had to slowly befriend and get to know each other. And, most importantly, they had to find a way to jointly make the case for their respective challenges and produce synergies and joint solutions. Unsurprisingly, this led to controversy when it came to balancing and weighing development versus environment, how much growth, industrialization, and infrastructure was needed, in particular in poor countries, versus protecting animals, plants, and the climate. On all sides, an unprecedented learning process set in about how inextricably linked fighting poverty and protecting the environment was, and how much the economy played a role in almost all areas. There was no denying anymore that a thorough transformation of prevailing growth and prosperity models had to happen all over the world, and there was no country, neither rich nor poor, that could claim already being there. Hence, this time it was not about some countries that should be enabled to catch up with the rest of the world, like in the MDG era, but it was about a global transformation of an unprecedented scale that should happen everywhere. And the SDGs were supposed to be the path leading to this brave new sustainable world. However, the fact that there was no specific example to follow as truly sustainable living and working models were still in the making, complicated things even more.

This chapter will scrutinize how all of these hard-to-digest new insights and hard-to-reconcile caveats unavoidably left their traces in the goals and targets. Sometimes the delegations produced only halfway thought-through wordings, oblivious of crucial impediments or repercussions, sometimes the delegations were lost in politics and eventually not going much beyond general recommendations or even leaving blanks. But sometimes astonishingly innovative and ambitious goals and targets were devised, pinpointing to the neuralgic points decisive for the future of humanity and the planet. Subsequently, the "2030 Agenda for Sustainable Development" ended up with a mixed result of goals and targets: some of them were ambitious, comprehensive, and innovative, while others remained weak, contradictory, or leaving many aspects wide open to interpretation.

When a new agreement of such far-reaching implications is set up, inevitably the question of how to finance these new undertakings comes up. This will be covered by the final part of this chapter. The separate Financing for Development (FfD) track was tasked to negotiate a new financing agreement, tied to the 2030 Agenda. The debate was essentially boiling down to three key questions: how to significantly increase levels of funding, how to broaden the variety of sources of funding, and how to ensure that the money spent would yield the desired results. All of this would be urgently needed, given the level of ambition and scope of the 2030 Agenda. Discussing the financing of the SDGs was happening against the backdrop of a fundamentally different development reality compared to the MDG era. The once sharp dividing line between donors and recipients was getting increasingly blurred with long-time recipients becoming donors themselves, and financial flows from capital markets to the Global South dwarfing traditional aid. In addition, the envisaged merging of the poverty and environmental agenda was producing many sensitivities. In particular the poor countries feared that development finance would lose out against environment and climate finance, thus leading to an overall reduced financial support to them. Similarly, as with the SDGs, negotiating the financing agenda was shaped by a lot of vitriol and controversy, and the by the FfD track in July 2015 reached agreement, the Addis Ababa Action Agenda, equally ended up with a very mixed result.

Finally, looking back at those three years and three months between the Rio Conference 2012, mandating the SDGs, and the UN Development Summit 2015, adopting the SDGs, this chapter will also take a closer look at the political footprints the post-2015 process left. It will explore how this process upended and put into question long-time held beliefs and tenets about the role model of rich countries that couldn't be an example anymore, about the full impact of economic development that wouldn't only bring blessings but both boon and bane, and about the relationship between developed and developing countries and outlived traditional donor-recipient relations. Political compromise and concession, economic constraints and election cycles, the political momentum and readiness to start into a new sustainable era inevitably all left their traces in the new agenda. Looking at the post-2015 process in hindsight to better grasp the nature of the SDGs helps understanding where politics came in the way of science or vice versa, where the best intentions clashed with realpolitik and economics, or with the fear to be on the losing end or to not fit into this new SDG world.

The equally complex implementation of this new agenda and the 17 goals and 169 targets will be scrutinized in Chapter 4. This chapter is not a detailed stocktaking and an in-depth analysis of where the single goals and targets stand as there are other regular reports and more up-to-date resources about SDG progress. Instead, it will be focusing on overarching topics and aspects that play a key role in putting the SDGs into practice and that are decisive for the implementation of the whole agenda.

During the post-2015 negotiations, right from the start, the availability or rather dearth of data was a heatedly debated topic. While delegations were afraid of ending up with a system, either too watered-down, low in ambition and, thus, meaningless, or too complex, high in ambition and, thus, unmanageable, the statistical community had to tread unbeaten paths, anyway. Many new issues, like human rights, inequality, governance, or inclusive societies, appearing as rather political and not measurable, triggered considerable controversy, how they should be incorporated, if at all. The delegations being critical, often argued with their political nature and, thus, the impossibility to draft meaningful goals and targets about human rights or governance. The political haggling over the SDGs also had produced some fuzzy or overloaded targets that were the result of some face-saving compromise or of incorporating and satisfying differing perspectives. Unsurprisingly, the final set of the indicator framework, eventually comprising 226 indicators, to measure progress on the SDGs or lack of thereof, was full of compromises and also blanks that couldn't be filled. Thus, this part of the chapter will examine the indicator framework, its strengths and weaknesses in delivering sound results on assessing progress. Considering that the SDG indicators were the first set of this kind to comprehensively measure sustainability, the chapter will also take a deep look into what assessing and measuring sustainability in general means, a tremendously underestimated challenge, and how the statistical community has advanced in this field since 2015.

As the SDGs were the result of merging the poverty and the environmental agenda, they had to deal with a bunch of so-called wicked problems. Typically, these entail conflicting aims that render any easy and uncontested solution almost impossible, for example, reconciling the goals on growth or industrialization with the goals on protecting the environment and the climate. Often, there is a trade-off that has to be managed by politicians and other actors. The 2030 Agenda entails most of those wicked challenges but does not provide detailed answers how to reconcile more food, more economic prosperity, and employment with reducing the human footprint and protecting the environment. Identifying truly sustainable solutions, in fact, means weighing a myriad of factors that come into play. It also means to hit the moving target as there is still so much that science and research need to understand about the full impact of human action on ecosystems, about the human footprint on the planet, and about ways of effectively reducing it. Unsurprisingly, against this background, the SDGs could only be rather general or sketchy on many issues. Thus, this chapter will analyze the specific challenges about going sustainable in daily life and the repercussions for governments, the private sector, or consumers. It will examine where and how growth and wellbeing clash with protecting the environment, where politics clashes with science, and what tackling these wicked problems means for the SDGs and their implementation.

Another overarching key topic is the role of the private sector in the SDGs and in going sustainable. Although not being explicitly denoted so, the economy is, in fact, one of the linchpins of the 2030 Agenda and key for fighting poverty and protecting the environment. Neither eradicating poverty nor reaching a thorough economic transformation toward sustainable living and working models will happen without a strong buy-in by the private sector. Investment, innovation, and a comprehensive restructuring and reshaping of economic and business models are essential for moving toward sustainable economies. But this is not yet happening at the scale and speed needed. Hence, the focus of this part of the chapter will be on how to enable sustainable investing, sustainable growth, and sustainable consumption and production patterns to become the new normal. There is still a rather uneasy and distanced relationship between the poverty and the environmental communities on the one hand, and the business world on the other. Both communities often don't necessarily see themselves on the same side with the private sector where traditional share-holder value and maximizing profits are still dominating tenets. After all, companies are rather responding to consumers' choices and demands as well as to the framing conditions of making profits. But, nevertheless, there are remarkable developments that are pushing the business case for sustainability. While going sustainable was for many years perceived as possibly rather hurting profits and the business of philanthropies, those long-time dominating perceptions are changing and aspects of sustainability are increasingly shaping growth models and business strategies. Thus, this chapter will examine the relationship between profit and shareholder-value and the envisaged green economic transformation. It will also look into phenomena such as green-washing and green marketing to find out if the SDGs are providing the needed guidance for the economic dimensions of sustainable development and if they manage to reconcile profit and purpose.

Finally, the current state of play of the SDGs, unsurprisingly, reveals a very mixed and patchy picture which will be discussed in the final part of this chapter. There is a group of least-developed countries (LDCs) that remain trapped in cycles of entrenched poverty, unlikely to make any progress on the SDGs. The COVID-19 pandemic and the most recent wars in different parts of the world have nothing but further exacerbated hunger and food insecurity, ushering in record numbers of refugees and displaced persons, and even pushed people back into poverty. Although the rise of the middle-income countries (MICs) is living proof of that it is possible to lift millions of people out of poverty in a short period of time, there are no easy-to-replicate success formulas, working all across the world. Also, the harrowing flipside of catching up economically on the fast lane has led to devastating environmental degradation with skyrocketing air and water pollution and hazardous waste and residues threatening human health and natural ecosystems.

Worryingly, demography adds another layer to the mounting pressure. If the global population reaches between 9 and 10 billion people by 2050, and if the rate of poor people turning into middle-class consumers, living the Western high-consumption lifestyles, continues at the same speed and scale, the equivalent of several earths will soon be needed. The current projections are deeply troubling; there is too much pollution, degradation and depletion, and too little progress on environmental sustainability. Concurrently, rising food and energy demand of a growing population is set to inexorably drain the earth's ecosystems. It is unlikely that this ongoing global overshoot beyond planetary boundaries will go without dramatic impact on prosperity and wellbeing for humanity on earth. Thus, there is an increasing urgency to act to which the little progress on the SDGs is the alarming testimony.

Finally, Chapter 5 will put the threads together and summarize the lessons learned from living in the SDG era, so far. Since 2015, every year the SDG crowd meets in New York at the United Nations to discuss and analyze the state of play of the SDGs and to exchange about how to overcome shortcomings and accelerate progress. Contrary to the initial wariness of governments about potentially being grilled at the UN regarding progress or setbacks on the SDGs, most have developed an unexpected high enthusiasm and willingness to be part of the game and engage in debating a more sustainable world.

But all enthusiasm about participating in SDG debates and the voluntary reports by governments, clearly tilting toward emphasizing success stories, can't conceal that the reality on the ground about achieving the SDGs and going sustainable is deeply troubling. Without the impacts resulting from the pandemic and the most recent wars, much more progress, in particular regarding the fight against poverty, most probably would have been possible. But it's also true that eliminating poverty was already far off track before COVID-19 hit the world. For many years, there has been little to no progress in many LDCs. Thus, it is crucial to understand where the bottlenecks and the obstacles are when it comes to eradicating poverty in those places. Equally abysmal is the performance on the environmental goals that are projected to stay out of reach. The climate goal about limiting greenhouse gas emissions and achieving the 1.5-degree pledge remains clearly far off track, as the yearly climate conferences prominently and inexorably underscore.

Similarly worrying is the little progress regarding the envisaged economic transformation. The SDGs came to ignite a thorough transformation but undeniably this process is going through troubled water, facing many obstacles and impediments, and demanding much more political will, perseverance, and ingenuity than ever expected. Of course, not all is doom and gloom, but obviously things go awry, and with more than half of the implementation time elapsed, there is no way denying that this is not the comprehensive transformation at the speed and scale envisaged in 2015.

Going sustainable has, in fact, turned out to be an ongoing learning and adapting challenge. Now with SDG implementation in full swing, there is also a lot more insight into what the SDGs can potentially do and what not. Some shortcomings were already baked into the SDGs, resulting from their political creation process and the difficult endeavor of merging the poverty and the environmental agenda. Other weaknesses became apparent only later when governments, communities, and experts had to work with the goals and targets. After all, the 2030 Agenda, in fact, reflects what was politically possible in 2015 at the UN, but not necessarily what was scientifically or economically useful or desirable. And a couple of years later, with research and innovation rapidly advancing, and experience in sustainability growing, there is considerably more evidence and insight what propels sustainable development and what rather doesn't, and where there are the tough nuts to crack in finding and implementing sustainable solutions. Thus, looking into over a decade of SDG implementation, this chapter will draw conclusions on why the SDG promise about decent lives for all and a more sustainable world is far off track. It will conclude where the SDGs opened up new avenues, spurred exploring many unbeaten paths, and what is left of the plan to save the world. When the SDGs came into this world, enthusiasm and confidence about building a better future prevailed. But the UN had seen enthusiasm before, and moving from words to action has always been tedious and frustrating. Thus, this final chapter will analyze what to learn from other UN agreements, the potential and leverage of legally binding agreements in advancing an agenda, and how the time until 2030 could be used most effectively for advancing the SDGs.

Finally, this chapter will venture out into the open, and with the 2030 deadline in sight look beyond the SDGs into the time after. It is highly likely that there will be something following the 2030 Agenda; anything else would be highly surprising and likewise disappointing. The world more than ever needs a plan to secure a decent future worthwhile living for all. As time is running out for humanity and the planet, it is crucial to look into post-2030 with an unequivocal focus on producing action and results. There are several options thinkable, just extending the deadline for the SDGs, updating and tweaking the goals and targets or completely opening them up and negotiating a new framework. Many arguments point toward having a leaner and more focused agenda. Discussing some of these ideas in this concluding chapter will hopefully serve to generate some inspirational input and forward-looking proposals for what could and should follow the SDGs and what to expect and demand from a post-2030 era.

Reference

United Nations (2023): *The Sustainable Development Goals Report 2023*, New York.

2

UNDERSTANDING THE ORIGINS OF THE SDGs

Going sustainable morphs from a supposed luxury into a question of survival

Facing an inconvenient truth: There is something deeply wrong with the prevailing growth model

It is humanity's most important relationship, but equally a complex and broken one, full of inspiration and insights, but also misunderstandings, denials, and ignorance: the relationship with the natural world. Human life since the beginning was characterized by a perpetual lack and by a constant struggle to satisfy basic livelihoods and respond to adverse living conditions and threats. Early humans were intimately and inextricably connected to nature – they had to as understanding, anticipating, and reacting to nature decided about life and death. The agricultural revolution marked a turning point in history as settling down and domesticating plants and animals led to the development of larger populations and civilizations and, also, a growing separation from the natural world. Interestingly, the more human societies developed, the more the relationship with nature changed, nurturing a perception of humankind having to overcome and dominate nature to lead a better life.

The Industrial Revolution eventually led to economy and population dynamics taking off. The steam engine and the use of fossil fuels opened up new economic possibilities that no one had even dared dreaming of before. Central to this development was coal, leading to new industries and new markets that propelled innovation, disruption, and invention. It was thrusting some parts of the world on a revolutionary accelerated development path with unprecedented growth. The age of industrialization dramatically changed the way economies were functioning, cities were built, labor was organized and business, trade, and commerce were done. New technologies opened up manifold new options for wage earning, producing convenient goods and services, and increasing

DOI: 10.4324/9781032702681-2

agricultural output. Travel, trade, and commerce became accessible for common people and were going to scale.

This period was igniting the most fundamental changes and disruptions ever in human history. The Industrial Revolution was at breathtaking speed upending traditional living and working patterns that had been shaping human lives for centuries. Cities sprouted and thrived, and people in large numbers moved to places where factories were mushrooming, offering all types of new jobs. In particular, the steam engine was a gamechanger, decisively propelling global industrialization, urbanization, and transportation. Later, the availability of reliable and cheap electricity transformed virtually every industrial activity. Skyrocketing economic growth, technological progress, and innovation seemed to be the new normal. People were becoming workers, while machines were subsequently replacing first animal and then human labor. The character and meaning of work underwent a thorough redefinition with many people taking over many rather dull tasks, not with the aim of producing something they would need for their own subsistence or trade, but instead taking home a certain amount of money. The colonies overseas were feeding the new industries in Europe and then America with resources and raw materials, fueling the manufacturing of all sorts of traditional and new goods. International trade was connecting very different places and cultures, facilitating the provision of raw material, workforce, and goods, and pulling up competition and consumption to a new level.

Amidst all this irrevocably reshaping of human lives, some other almost unnoticed transformation was also happening, and that was the relationship with nature. Before the Industrial Revolution, people in agricultural society were working for good harvests that largely depended on the weather and the natural environment. Natural resources then were only of value, if they were easy to reach and use. But with new technologies and machines, mostly running on cheap and abundant coal, much of this changed profoundly: factories were producing regardless of the weather and environmental conditions, coal and other energy-rich resources could now be easily tapped into and put to use. Efficiency and productivity were the new measures; distance became less relevant, and new goods and products were manufactured at scale and in a fracture of the time compared to handmade goods. Subsequently, a psychological change set in; with the growing confidence in the ability to use natural resources, there was a growing confidence in the ability to control nature and, thus, control life itself. "..., [T]echnology allowed Europeans to reach the long-desired goal of successfully dominating and 'overcoming' the natural world. Or so it seemed" (Caradonna 2014: 64–65).

With the Industrial Revolution unfolding, human progress claimed a new meaning. It was increasingly linked to economic growth and material advancement as the ways to reduce human dependence on the vicissitudes of nature and, thus, enable a better and safer life. There was a strong belief in science making use of the natural world through mastering new technologies and skills. This would free humanity from limitations and scarcities of the natural world that used to characterize human life. Combined with intellectual advances of individual rights, the law and spiritual cultivation, this would not only open up avenues to unprecedented comfort and possibilities, but also enable the exercise of individual freedom. This type of human progress, born in the Western world and spread by the Western world, was supposed to bring progress to the whole world. Taming wild nature and making the earth a more inhabitable and controllable place could only be intrinsically good and desirable, so the general assumption of those that drove and benefited from the Industrial Revolution.

Thriving and growing became possible through human hands; the more something was man-made, the more it stood for progress. Nature and the environment were largely seen as a boundless source of resources and raw material and as a dump ground for anything that was left over or that was a useless by-product. In Western intellectual circles in the 18th and the 19th centuries, the notion of advancement and progress was widely perceived as faith in the ability and capability of humankind to determine its own destiny. Some studies also found a prevailing attitude of people at the time believing in a right to dominate and exploit nature for the sake of maximizing profits and affluence. If this kind of advancement and progress was possible and enabled so many people to lead a better life on earth, how could it possibly be wrong (Du Pisani 2006: 83–85)?

The age of industrialization was largely shaped by a lot of optimism, a firm belief in human ingenuity to fix any possible negative repercussions and to further advance and perfect whatever was not working in the desired way. But in hindsight, the legacy of the Industrial Revolution is rather contested and mixed. The downside and many negative long-term effects were fully revealed only many years later. One crucial long-term impact, initially, was hardly noticeable and imaginable, but then became increasingly conspicuous: taming and cultivating nature slowly but steadily turned into depleting, polluting, extinguishing, and causing irreversible environmental damage. A laissez-faire capitalism, fueling consumption, exploitation, and unregulated growth, led not only to severe environmental degradation but also negative impacts on people's wellbeing and health due to dire living and working conditions. Nevertheless, it took a long way to realize that something was deeply wrong with the way economic growth was pursued and spread over the world. And this type of growth carried a long tail with heavy, long-lasting ecological and social repercussions with it.

The Industrial Revolution was the ignition sequence and the accelerator leading to an age of rampant growth and overconsumption. It was a tremendous economic, social, and ecological turmoil, a new chapter in human and environmental history, thoroughly altering many of the earth's landscapes and societies in Europe and North America. Industrialization also led to the rise of fossil fuels to superpower status, establishing a global fossil energy regime to last until today. The environmental impact appeared as negligible or at least manageable in the long run.

Interestingly, criticism of this new age of industrialization and growth was already emerging at the time of its heydays, challenging the assumption of producing overall benefits and of all people happily enjoying this progress. Economists, political activists, and scientists, witnessing the unfolding Industrial Revolution in the 18th and 19th century, were critical of pollution, inequality, and unsustainable growth that seemed rather unsuitable as the basis for prosperity and wellbeing for the present and future generations. Skyrocketing mass consumption and production had already at the time led to a visible reduction of crucial resources, such as timber or coal, which made once unthinkable depletion scenarios realistic and possible. Analyzing the confluence of accelerated industrial production and population growth, intellectuals and economists already at the time were raising the idea that certain natural limits should not be overstepped and natural resources should not be overexploited. Otherwise, economies and societies were unlikely to flourish and thrive in the long run. Growth based on coal as a finite non-renewable resource, would obviously not generate prosperity any more, once this energy source was exhausted. But understanding the importance of functioning ecological cycles as being indispensable for human wellbeing and prosperity was only in its infancy (Caradonna 2014: 81–83; Charbonnier 2021: 83–85; Du Pisani 2006: 86–87). An increasingly heavy and visible impact of the age of industrialization on nature, people, and life itself, in fact, were sowing the seeds of doubt about human ingenuity being able to pave the way for a brighter future by subjugating and exploiting nature. As a result, this led to first discussions about sustainability and a sustainable use of resources.

The daunting and worrying impact of overstepping natural limits first became an issue in the forest and timber business. Forest management out of necessity became a trailblazer in exploring ideas of sustainability. Timber was a key resource in the 17th and 18th centuries in many European countries and later North America, needed for firewood, building houses, fueling factories, or constructing ships. A possible shortage would have a widespread impact on the growing population and industries. And such a scenario wasn't unfounded as the growing need for fire and energy had led to a worrying degree of deforestation in many places. At the beginning of the 18th century about 85 percent of Massachusetts was covered with forests, by 1870 it was only 30 percent. Foresters in England, France, and Germany started publishing books about how to conserve and cultivate timber in a way that would allow a continued, steady and sustained use. Authors, such as John Evelyn or Hanns Carl von Carlowitz, were discussing the economic and social forces driving deforestation and an overuse of resources, that were irresponsibly ignoring the economic and social impact on future generations (Du Pisani 2006: 85–86; Grober 2007: 8–15; Smil 2017: 165–166).

However, the mainstream narrative of modern economic history for a long time kept on praising the impressive rise of the Western world due to its technological and institutional ingenuity as the core and linchpin of the Industrial Revolution. This narrative lopsidedly defined modernity as the unfolding ability of humankind to produce and consume an unprecedented amount of energy, while mostly staying silent on the environmental and social costs and the role of conquest, colonization, slavery, and exploitation. Many economic historians tended to underscore the conclusion that the Industrial Revolution stood, in fact, for overcoming the dependencies and laws made by nature and achieving a certain liberation. Despite some hardship for some parts of society, this period was rather seen as an era enabling humankind to take much of its destiny into its own hands, enabling far more people than ever to earn a profit and lead a good life. Only in the 1980s and 1990s, ecological critics started to challenge these narratives on a broader scale and fill the gaps about the socio-environmental costs of the Industrial Revolution (Barca 2011; Charbonnier 2021: 22–23).

In the 20th century, especially the plenty of the post-World War decades with the spreading availability of many materials and resources, propelled low cost and mass production of everyday-day goods. These led to the high-consumption lifestyles that became part of Western culture. After years of war and totalitarianism, focusing on human and social rights and enabling a higher standard of living for the masses, also helped leaving behind the times of World War II. In particular, the 1950s and 1960s with unprecedented growth rates fostered a belief in unlimited growth and ever-increasing affluence eventually reaching all those across the world that were still living in poverty and destitution. Possible negative repercussions on resources or the environment were either put aside as not of primary concern or with the belief that these would soon be met by new technologies and new products (Charbonnier 2021: 172–173; Du Pisani 2006: 87–88). During this period, the use of artificial substances proliferated, ranging from household cleaners, industrial synthetic chemicals to agricultural pesticides, herbicides, and other new substances. These were often used without any precautionary testing or regulation, due to little awareness that these might have severe impacts on health and the environment (McNeill/Engelke 2014: 136).

The many tangible benefits of growth, resulting in a growing middle class in the Western world, seemed to proof all those right chasing after growth. In 1820, globally the majority of people lived in extreme poverty and only a small elite enjoyed higher living standards. But with economic growth, decisively spurred by the Industrial Revolution, poverty rates had been continuously falling over the last two centuries. This is especially remarkable as the world population increased seven-fold over the same period. For the past 200 years, growth and modernization kept on creating wealth and prosperity in the Western world although with highly unequal distribution ratios within societies.

Eventually, in the 1960s, human impact on the earth's ecosystems was receiving increasing scientific attention, accompanied by rising political activism and the establishment of new environmental organizations. One key work in this regard was "Silent Spring" by Rachel Carson in 1962, disclosing the dangers posed to humans and wildlife by an indiscriminate overuse of pesticides (Carson 1962). Another groundbreaking piece was "The Tragedy of the Commons" by Garrett Hardin in 1968, dramatically underscoring that air, water, and soil were commons that couldn't be used at will without any restrictions as their regenerating and recovering capacities were limited. His warning against greed, ignorance, and apathy and a deadly ill-advised attitude toward nature as a resource and service free of charge triggered a critical debate regarding many commonly established views on the environment and how overuse and depletion could best be curbed (Hardin 1968).

The Founex report on Development and Environment from 1971, an NGO report, was the first paper to cogently discuss critical interlinkages between development and the environment as two sides of the same coin. The report alerted that the development path of the rich countries had led to too much depletion and pollution. Thus, regarding the rich countries as the model to emulate was rather ill-advised as this would only accelerate and spread environmental degradation. However, given the deep ideological and political rift between industrialized and developing countries at the time, shaped by years of decolonization and founding of new nations, poor countries were deeply suspicious that environmental issues would be used as a pretext to keep them mired in poverty and underdevelopment. Hence, the report concluded "that it is for the developed countries to reassure the developing world that their growing environmental concern will not hurt the continued development of the developing world...." Considering that the report dates from 1971, scientific understanding about sustainability and causes and remedies regarding environmental degradation was rather limited. Hence, the authors openly acknowledged the "uncertain stage of our knowledge regarding the interaction of environmental and development policies" (Founex Report 1971).

A major milestone and a turning point in bringing the world together on the environmental challenges was the World Conference on the Human Environment in Stockholm in 1972. It was the first international meeting debating potentially contradictory conflicting aims between development and protecting the environment. Unsurprisingly, the question of responsibility stirred much vitriol. The developing countries had come to Stockholm rather reluctantly. In their view, industrialized countries bore the sole responsibility as they had reached industrialization and prosperity through plundering natural resources and polluting air and water. Now, the rich countries were asking the poor countries to share the burden and, thus, willfully ignoring that they didn't have any share in the benefit and prosperity. The rich countries' alleged concern about preventing any adding up to the environmental damage was only a pretext for further enhancing uneven economic relations and trade patterns. The real goal was to thwart the poor countries' trajectory to reach a similar prosperity level, so the suspicion by the developing countries. They regarded caring about environmental issues a luxury they couldn't and wouldn't afford. The statement from Ivory Coast that they would prefer even more pollution as this was obviously proof of development and progress strikingly reflected the view on development and the environment at the time (Sanwal 2015: 72–73).

Despite all reluctance and wariness, the Stockholm conference managed to agree on some at the time quite revolutionary conclusions, stating that the time had come to change course: "A point has been reached in history when we must shape our actions throughout the world with a more prudent care for their environmental consequences. Through ignorance or indifference we can do massive and irreversible harm to the earthly environment on which our life and well-being depend" (United Nations 1973: 3). The Stockholm outcome didn't explicitly define or refer to sustainable development, but agreed to the notion that both development and the environment should be managed in a mutually beneficial way. With Stockholm, the environment had entered the international stage: it had made its debut as a bone of contention as well as a common challenge, affecting the whole world and, thus, demanding global solutions.

Also in 1972, the think tank "Club of Rome" published its best-selling piece "The Limits to Growth," a watershed moment that triggered a heated debate about the price of continuously chasing after growth. The study advocated for a new approach to economics and growth, arguing that only respecting ecological limits would enable society to avoid possible doomsday scenarios. The environment had to become part of the equation of human life; limiting and regulating human activity was indispensable. The prevailing growth model of the West, supposedly a model for wellbeing and prosperity, was increasingly and relentlessly backfiring, propelling apocalyptic scenarios for the whole world, so the bitter conclusion (Charbonnier 2021: 191–198; Du Pisani 2006: 90–93).

The report, "Our Common Future," by the World Commission on Environment and Development in 1987, also called Brundtland report after the former Norwegian prime minister and chair of the commission, was one of the first to recognize the conundrum of sustainable development: poor countries were seeking growth to eradicate poverty but were pursuing a fatally flawed growth model, as lived by the example of rich countries. The result was environmental degradation, unequal prosperity, and depletion of resources. All these already daunting prospects were set to further deteriorate with a rapidly growing population and many more millions of poor people wanting to escape poverty. To the surprise of many, the report also called for involving the private sector, acknowledging that corporations were the engines of global growth and development, thus, they had to be at the heart of any solution (World Commission on Environment and Development 1987).

The report was one of the first trying to strike a balance between the conflicting aims of leaving behind poverty and protecting the environment by spelling out the famous sentence that would be the cue and tenet for many years to come: ensuring that the needs of the present generations were met without compromising the ability of future generations to meet their own needs. The report has, in fact, set the tone for international development policy since the 1980s and decisively propelled debates about reconciling economic growth, environmental protection, and social inequality without causing damage to the respective other realm. It was quite open about the devastating repercussions of rampant economic growth, focusing on maximizing profit and share-holder value. These economic development models were consistently neglecting nature as a factor in the human economic equation and, thus, sowing the seeds of its own demise (Lucatello 2017: 202–203; Palmer 1992: 1010–1011).

Scientists and journalists in the early 21st century would eventually use the term "Anthropocene" for describing the earth age that is largely shaped by human activity and its impact on the earth (McNeill/Engelke 2014: 204–205). Thus, this new age obviously required a new global environmental agenda. However, what exactly this should look like and what it should do remained rather unclear. The only certainty was that there was something deeply wrong with the prevailing growth model as it was threatening future generations to live and thrive on earth. And, as underscored in the Brundtland report, it was the responsibility of the present generations to do something about it.

From Rio 1992 to Rio 2012: The global plan for the environment

Firmly determined to set up a new framework for humanity assuming its responsibility for sustainable life on earth, in June 1992, the world came together at the first and rather famous United Nations Conference on Environment and Development. Hosted by Brazil, the Rio Earth Summit, as it became known, was the largest environmental conference ever held until then, and attracted over 30,000 participants, including more than 100 heads of state and hundreds of NGOs. Building on the Brundtland report and its warnings, the conference aimed at identifying responses to pressing global environmental challenges and outlining ways for humanity to prosper within planetary boundaries.

An initially very enthusiastic run-up to the summit had ignited high hopes and expectations, in particular in civil society and the scientific community about a possible new international environmental law with an effective institutional set-up to ensure implementation. The UN Secretary-General Boutros Boutros-Ghali boldly declared in his opening that this summit would define the state of the political will to save the planet. However, the debates very quickly became controversial and incriminatory between the Global South and the Global North, but also between governments and civil society. They were basically clashing about the interlinkages between development, the economy and environment, about how much production and consumption the earth could sustain, population growth and its impact on natural ecosystems or about who had to take over how much responsibility for environmental damages and the subsequent consequences. Unsurprisingly, many governments preferred dodging any impediment to their own development and prospering, anything that could possibly restrict their own decision-making in economics or the environment. For example, the US and the Europeans were protecting their biochemical companies, the

Arab countries were protecting their gas and oil companies, and Brazil and Malaysia rejected any restrictions on the use and exploitation of their tropical forests, with the Malaysian Prime Minister even accusing the Global North that, "[at] Rio, eco-imperialism prevailed" (Mahathir bin Mohamed 1999; Little 1995: 271–272).

Throughout the negotiations, the focus of the developing countries was on poverty eradication and socio-economic progress as their first and foremost priorities. Environmental impact was rather seen as something that could be dealt with later, as long as it did not hamper economic growth. Similarly, the developed countries were keen on protecting and defending their high-consumption lifestyles, but concurrently advocating for more environmental protection. The bitter disagreements were largely about what kind of development was needed to lift the poor out of poverty and how much more fast but environmentally harmful fossil-fuel based development the environment could tolerate or rather should endure given the high numbers of people still in poverty. In a nutshell, the main beef of contention was which agenda was more important and required more immediate action and what kind of action: fighting poverty or protecting the environment. But tellingly, the discussion about lifestyles, growth, and prosperity wasn't that clearly dividing developed and developing countries. Despite all the downsides and growing scientific evidence that this was unsustainable, it was still the aspired living model that rich countries didn't want to give up and poor countries wanted to reach.

Frustratingly, the Earth Summit outcome couldn't land anywhere close to what was deemed necessary from a scientific point of view for effectively protecting the environment and preventing further damage. From the beginning, a lack of leadership, political commitment and preparation had failed any ambition or hope for a far-reaching agreement. "Growth remained the imperative. Humans first, and no-holds-barred development to enable developing countries to catch up with the others" (Caballero/Londoño 2022: 8). Aspects of sustainability and long-term negative human impact were at least referenced but the dominating mantra was growth and prosperity and not challenging any comforts of lifestyle.

Nevertheless, Rio 1992 produced some crucial outcome documents: two legally binding agreements, the "UN Framework Convention on Climate Change" (UNFCCC) and the "Convention on Biological Diversity" (CBD), that were, in fact, already agreed on before Rio and just incorporated into the summit, and three legally non-binding agreements, the "Agenda 21," the "Rio Declaration," and the "Statement of Forest Principles." The UNFCCC and the CBD only managed to go through as legally binding because of watered-down language, often demanded by the US, and leaving out many crucial points. The climate convention, for example, was missing any targets on the reduction of emissions of greenhouse gases (Little 1995: 269–270; Palmer 1992: 1006–1008). Nevertheless, in hindsight, these two agreements were landmark conventions and first crucial steps toward a comprehensive sustainable development agenda later to come.

"Rio produced too little, too late," so the deeply disappointed and disillusioned summary of the former Minister for the Environment and Prime Minister of New Zealand (Palmer 1992: 1028). Even the Secretary-General of the Earth Summit was outspoken about the disappointingly weak language and little commitment in almost every regard (Strong 1992). But considering that the UN was seen by many member states rather as the arena for peace and security, most of them were quite reluctant anyway about too much regulation and intervention from the UN in areas they deemed as their national prerogative. Only die-hard enthusiasts and environmentalists could have expected some full-fledged international environmental law coming out of Rio. Nevertheless, it was the first time that in the framework of the UN, the traditional way to prosperity and wellbeing was not only openly put into question, but also increasingly perceived as a broken model, full of enticing promises in the short run but full of destruction and devastation in the long run.

But despite all disagreement and bickering, the unprecedented public attention and extensive media coverage of the Rio summit, contributed considerably to raising awareness about the pressing sustainability challenges. Since Rio, sustainable development has been a key part of the international agenda. But it would take more years and more alarming reports until environmental issues would usher in specific action. The UNFCCC climate agenda was a frontrunner in this regard, paving the way for targeted climate action through the annual COP (Conference of the Parties) climate meetings, starting in 1995.

Regrettably, one long-lasting, burdening legacy from Rio was a very politized perception of environmental protection and environmental policy, with the developed and the developing countries squarely opposing each other and disagreeing about many issues. The geopolitical upheavals happening at the time were further kindling the divisions: The Rio summit in 1992 took place at a crossroads where the allegiances of the Cold War were falling apart. Developing countries didn't see themselves being forced any more to choose sides in a once dominating East–West scenario, and the G-77, the UN group of the developing countries comprising 125 countries at the time, were subsequently emerging as a powerful bloc at the UN. They were asserting their voice in international negotiations louder than ever before and insisting on the obligation of the rich countries to support the poor (Palmer 1992: 1020–1021).

Despite all disappointment, the aftermath of Rio with the various new agreements in place was a call to action for the United Nations. UN Secretary-General Kofi Annan was happy to heed the call and initiated the Millennium Ecosystem Assessment (MEA), producing several reports between 2001 and 2006. The objectives of these reports were to assess the consequences of ecosystem change for human wellbeing and to identify the action needed for protecting and using those systems in a sustainable way. This work involved more than 1,360 experts worldwide who came to devastating conclusions, sounding many alarm bells. In their key findings they pointed out that over the past 50 years, humans have changed ecosystems more rapidly and extensively than in any comparable period in human history. Main drivers were rapidly growing demands for food, fresh water, timber, fiber, and fuel. While intensifying and scaling up agriculture, industrial and energy production and infrastructure had helped to improve the lives of billions, nature's ability to deliver key services, such as purifying air and water or providing resources, was increasingly hampered. The first and foremost change that had to happen was in human attitude and action. As long as nature and its ecosystems were perceived as free and limitless, humanity would most likely continue on this destructive path, at the end of the day threatening human wellbeing itself, so the reports (Millennium Ecosystem Assessment 2001–2001).

With a view to the many interlinkages between eradicating poverty and protecting the environment, evidence was suggesting that the poverty and environmental agendas should go hand in hand, bringing the respective policies together. The once cherished prosperity model of the rich countries could under no circumstances be the model to follow for the poor countries anymore, so the conclusions of the experts.

The Rio follow-up summit in Johannesburg ten years later, the Earth Summit 2002, also known as Rio+10, was a largely powerless event as with the US a major player was missing. There was little hope anyway, that the US would engage in the environmental agenda any time soon as the Bush administration not only openly rejected the summit itself but also refused deep-cutting measures to curb CO_2 emissions. In addition, the more than unfortunate timing of Rio+10 didn't help the cause. In the wake of the 9/11 terrorist attacks on the US in 2001, major Western countries were absorbed by the only recently started US war on terror and the controversies about the looming US-led war against Iraq, starting the following year. During those major geopolitical upheavals, ambitious results in development and environmental policies were unlikely and unrealistic right from the start.

In its "Growth Report" from 2008, the Commission on Growth and Development, a multidisciplinary group of experts, set up by the World Bank, attempted to distill what had been learned in the past decades about growth and development. The idea that poor countries should or could to some extent emulate the strategies of the rich countries to catch up was clearly dismissed. The Commission warned that "most developing countries decide to grow first and worry about the environment later. This is a costly mistake" (Commission on Growth and Development 2008: 65). In the end, it would be cheaper to not make these mistakes in the first place. Interestingly, the report was reshuffling the traditional blame game between the Global North and the Global South, underscoring that the dividing line between those causing environmental problems and those suffering was turning increasingly blurred. Developing countries could no longer be seen as mere victims of climate change. Especially fast-growing economies, like China and India, were already generating too much carbon dioxide themselves to be ignored as part of the problem. China's annual emissions at the time were already matching those of the US. Thus, any climate action could only succeed, if the fast-growing developing economies were ready to take over their share of responsibility (Commission on Growth and Development 2008: 86–88). However, the report was also somewhat cautious and hesitant to dash all ambitions to grow, stressing that growth was still the best way to free people from poverty.

When getting ready for the next Conference on Sustainable Development in Rio in 2012, popularly known as Rio+20, many governments were in a rather bleak mood about what to expect. There was no denying that in the 20 years elapsed since the first Rio summit in 1992, the world's state of the environment had continued to deteriorate: the global demand for natural resources had doubled and was now 50 percent higher than the regenerative capacity of the planet. Carbon emissions had increased by 40 percent, biodiversity loss was accelerating, and the pressure on ecosystems was set to further rapidly intensify with a global population projected to rise to 9 billion by 2015.

Negotiations on the first draft of the later outcome document "The Future We Want" of the Rio+20 summit started in January 2012. And it should be an arduous and painful journey. Over the weeks and months, the draft was growing in pages and topics that member states, entangled in highly politicized and time-consuming negotiations, wanted to see reflected in the document. The whole process became even more convoluted as the facilitators for the negotiations established around 14 splinter groups that would negotiate different parts of the draft outcome in parallel. It was increasingly difficult to see where the negotiations stood.

At some point, the discussions seemed to be spiraling out of control, as was the whole process. The first draft that had started with 19 pages and 65 paragraphs had burgeoned to more than 200 pages and 420 paragraphs with the vast majority of them being contested and disputed. There was a high level of distrust and acrimony, frustrating delegations to the point that a failure seemed almost unavoidable (Caballero/Londoño 2022: 99–112).

In June 2012, the Rio Sustainable Development Conference was officially kicked off, celebrating the 20-year anniversary of the Rio Earth Summit. Again, it was a mega-summit, the biggest UN event so far, with 130 heads of state and government and more than 45,000 participants attending. The 10-day summit was supposed to renew and foster global commitment to the three dimensions of sustainable development: economic, social, and the environment, and to set the agenda for the next 20 years. But it was no happy anniversary, much to the contrary.

As the tedious and painful negotiations on the outcome document had been dragging on since January, the whole event was marked by disappointed, disillusioned, wary, and lamenting interventions, delegations putting the blame on each other for lack of progress on what was agreed in Rio 1992. The rooms were filled with participants, issuing the usual recriminations, and openly disagreeing about how to move on with the environmental agenda. Developing countries continued to insist that they needed financial and technological transfers from developed countries to attain higher levels of environmental protection, while deflecting criticism of their domestic practices and flawed policies that had spurred environmental degradation. And developed countries, likewise deflecting from their own flawed policies, insisted on the need for every country to engage in protecting the environment and refused a wildcard for poor countries. The conference was threatened to get stuck in a deadlock.

The developed countries were pushing the topic on transitioning to a green economy, based on renewable energy that should replace the brown economy, based on fossil fuels. As expected, this caused much heated debate not only between developing and developed countries but also between governments of industrialized countries and civil society. Different interpretations and definitions of what a green economy entailed, including controversial views on social and economic impact, caused much vitriol over burden-sharing and the relationship between environmental protection and poverty alleviation. Many emerging economies didn't want to leave the fast lane of economic development that was finally bearing the long-desired fruit, enabling millions of poor people to climb up the ladder of wellbeing at an unprecedented speed. If those emerging economies were now forced to switch from cheap fossil fuels to other more expensive forms of energy, chances were high that their economic engines would stutter and slow down. In addition, the developing countries were wary that promoting a green economy would be used as a pretext for additional trade restrictions and customs, giving European and American energy companies an advantage in the competition over becoming the global energy providers of the future. In the same vein, there was also much leery eyebrow-raising regarding the presence of 200 business CEOs in Rio. The idea was to involve the business world in common efforts regarding protecting the environment. But in particular civil society saw them rather as the problem and not the solution.

But amid disappointment, division, and entrenched positions, the delegates, decisively nudged by a courageous and skillful Brazilian host, took the chance to undertake a leap of faith. After numerous deliberations and discussions, they had come to the conclusion that the environmental agenda and the poverty agenda had to become one single agenda as they were basically two sides of the same coin. Deep transformation at an unprecedented scale was urgently needed across the world as the earth was facing historic and relentless degradation. At the same time, too many people remained mired in poverty and destitution. Thus, the environmental challenges couldn't be meaningfully tackled in isolation, nor could the social or the economic challenges. These three dimensions of development were inextricably intertwined; hence, an interlinked approach appeared the obvious thing to do. But merging two separate UN tracks was a highly disruptive undertaking that would meet considerable resistance in the very formal and protocol-driven UN world, full of strict rules, procedures, and hierarchies.

The ground for this rather bold move had been decisively prepared by Colombia that had been arguing and advocating since 2011 for global goals as possible successors to both the Rio process and the poverty agenda. The idea was to contrive a new set of goals that would be covering all critical aspects of sustainable development, a comprehensive framework, equally relevant for and applicable to all countries. Colombia, supported by a growing crowd of friends, set out on an informal long-term journey of relentlessly lobbying and promoting their concept. These new Sustainable Development Goals (SDGs) should be the successors to both the Millennium Development Goals (MDGs) of the poverty agenda, expiring in 2015, and the environmental agenda of the Rio process, in need of a successor agenda in 2012.

Initially, in first exchanges with other governments in 2011, this idea was bluntly dismissed as "ludicrous and utterly impractical" (Caballero/Londoño 2022: 25). Furthermore, any suggestion of giving up the MDGs or making them part of another agenda evoked considerable fears that this would severely cut into the fight against poverty, diverting attention and commitment from an unfinished, yet urgent business. Hence, the most outspoken group critical of possible SDGs were the African countries that feared MDG-based cooperation with Africa would be fatally undermined. Those opposing voices were rallying behind a vague concept named MDG+ that was supposed to maintain the basic MDG architecture as the linchpin of the development agenda. But this would have meant cementing a donor–recipient relationship in a world where many recipients had long outgrown that status and continuing with two separate agendas, one for the environment and one for poverty.

During the Rio negotiations, delegations were only very slowly opening up to this idea of a new framework, with both the process of getting there and the possible content triggering considerable vitriol. Regarding the process, most delegations wanted to stick with what they were familiar with and what they could control, and that was a standard intergovernmental UN format. However, Colombia and others feared that this business-as-usual would end up in highly politicized and little productive debates. Thus, they fought for taking politics out of the process and for setting up a body that would rather draw on technical expertise and experience and produce science-based recommendations. Governments were supposed to have only a minimal say.

Eventually, much against all odds, delegates grudgingly accepted the idea to not follow the usual UN rules but instead tread the unbeaten path of involving science, experts, and civil society to produce the new goals: the body to lead this new process was an Open Working Group (OWG). The OWG should consist of 30 members, six delegates from each of the five UN regional groups (Latin America and Caribbean, Western Europe and others, Eastern Europe, Africa, and Asia). The formal UN involvement would happen through member states formally starting the process in September 2012 and closing it in September 2015, respectively at the UN General Assembly and, thus, giving it the political sign-off and buy-in. With the OWG, the stage for a new game in the UN arena was set, but no one knew who would be holding the respective leading and supporting parts, and what a winning performance would look like.

Regarding the possible content, the OWG was eventually tasked with drafting a proposal for possible sustainable development goals as "a pathway for a sustainable century." The only further guidance delegates could agree on was that these envisaged "sustainable development goals should be action-oriented and easy to communicate, limited in number, aspirational, global in nature and universally applicable to all countries, while taking into account different national realities, capacities and levels of development and respecting national policies and priorities." They should include the three dimensions of sustainable development in balance with one another and focus on priority areas for the achievement of sustainable development. All relevant stakeholders and expertise from civil society, the scientific community, and the UN system should be fully involved in the process. Targets and indicators should be used for subsequently assessing progress on the goals. Anything else was left wide open to interpretation. Obviously, there was much room for rising up to the challenge and undertaking bold steps for a visionary powerful new agenda, but also much room for failing this idea.

After Rio, there was considerable criticism about the decision to set up a new agenda through merging the so far separate poverty and environmental tracks and adding the economic dimension. In fact, the Rio summit was often seen as a dismal failure as it had decided to give up the environmental track for something quite unknown and uncertain. There was "an atmosphere of distrust, tension and bickering," raising many doubts about the way ahead toward some vague all-encompassing sustainable development goals, as Olav Kjørven, at the time director at the United Nations Development Programme (UNDP), described it. He feared there was a good chance these new goals would be "doomed to drown in the quick sands of yet another complex process of negotiations at the UN" (Kjørven 2016). Some governments saw this endeavor very likely getting stuck in a dead end with a lot of potential for vitriol as this would sooner or later inevitably mean weighing which agenda was more important, eradicating poverty or protecting the environment. Painful compromises along the way would be unavoidable, so the general mood, poisoning the atmosphere for decades to come as both agendas were competing over public attention and financing. Civil society groups and the scientific community, though many of them embracing the idea of new sustainable development goals in principle, were equally scathing the outcome because of its vagueness, lack of detail, and ambition. Thus, deep suspicion was ubiquitous that in the end this process would produce a superficial and meaningless agenda with little impact, if at all, and see more losers than winners.

The year 2012, before and after the Rio summit was a frenzy, filled with debates, papers, and reports arguing for and against continuing with two tracks or merging them, weighing all sorts of potential arguments and pitfalls as well as benefits and catalyzing moments. In hindsight, the Rio decision was a valiant but also risky step, demanding a big leap of faith from everyone involved. It pushed the poverty community and the environmental community to reach out to each other, join hands and tread the unbeaten path of embarking on the journey of a new comprehensive sustainable development agenda, set to begin in 2015.

Looking back at Rio, despite a contested, uncertain and heavily criticized outcome, the 2012 summit outcome enabled the environmental agenda, after all, to liberate itself from a relatively frustrating existence. After two decades of heated debate and talk and very little action, reaching out to the poverty agenda also meant teaming up with the very popular and much better resourced poverty framework. Thus, the environmental community present in Rio was more open to this new proposal than the development community. Furthermore, the Rio+20 summit, due to its dimensions perceived as a "once-in-a-generation global event," was also a warning shot for the United Nations and its member states. If the Rio outcome was the best the world would possibly get from such a juggernaut process that in fact was only opening up the avenue to yet another process, this would sooner or later "represent the death knell for these overblown UN processes" (Bigg 2012). Thus, the OWG and the subsequent UN negotiations were under heavy pressure to do much better and deliver convincing and bold responses. No less than the credibility of the UN as a convening power for the world was at stake. It had to proof that it was able to bring member states together and provide the setting for overcoming entrenched differences, for effectively tackling global challenges and working for global solutions for a better world.

The Millennium Development Goals (MDGs): The global plan to fight poverty

In the 1960s, development and growth were quite a contested normative and ideological turf. Development ideologies were shaping the debates, Northern vs. Southern views, capitalist vs. socialist models, with many solidarity and decolonization movements vying for sympathy and support. But those debates were scarcely ushering in specific action.

This changed with the end of the Cold War and the East–West confrontations. In the 1990s, a new post-Cold War world took shape that initially relegated the development agenda to a back seat. The challenges following the demise of the Soviet Union were absorbing considerable political attention and financial resources. Concurrently, the Asian financial crisis in the 1990s sent rippling effects across the globe, and Latin America was reeling from its failed modernization efforts, mounting debt burdens and economic crises. Hunger and disaster in the poorest countries were swaying out of public awareness, and aid agencies, facing shrinking budgets, were increasingly losing clout to take effective action. The sidelined development community was feverishly looking for a way to get back into the limelight, remobilize public support for the fight against poverty and trigger renewed action.

To this end, in the 1990s, the UN held a series of development conferences, discussing key challenges and interlinkages between poverty, development and globalization. Subsequently, experts at the Development Assistance Committee (DAC) of the OECD, comprising 25 donors, and experts at the UN exchanged ideas about boiling down the essentials of fighting poverty to some basic numbers and clear messages. The result were two drafts: one from DAC experts, called International Development Goals (IDGs) and one from UN experts, called Internationally Agreed Development Goals (IADGs), both focusing on economic wellbeing, social development, and environmental sustainability (OECD 1996: 9–11). These two papers, for the first time, proposed translating fighting poverty into specific actionable goals.

One key figure shaping and revamping the development agenda was UN Secretary-General Kofi Annan. He made poverty eradication one central topic, and over the years development became the third pillar of the work at the UN, along with peace and security, and human rights. No longer stifled by East–West confrontations, the UN was seeking new room for action and unleash its potential for tackling global challenges. And a poverty and development agenda would be the perfect opportunity to unite and galvanize support from North, South, East, and West over the common, morally undisputable goal of fighting poverty. Annan's "perceived moral leadership was pivotal to reframing debates around a new spirit of partnership" (McArthur 2014: 6). One first major outcome was the Millennium Declaration, defining four priority areas and challenges for the 21st century: development and poverty, democracy and human rights, peace and security, and environmental protection. The declaration was particularly noteworthy for its clear and specific language, for listing commitments and quantitative goals that were easy to understand and that couldn't be altered through reinterpretation. It was adopted in September 2000 at the Millennium General Assembly, the doorstep to the 21st century and, thus, the occasion for the international community to symbolically enter a new era.

But despite the compelling language of the Millennium Declaration, the UN community was painfully aware of many UN declarations never having any real impact. Thus, to save the declaration from falling into oblivion, UN member states mandated Annan to draft a roadmap for implementation. He decided to bring together different actors of the development community, the bilateral donors through the OECD-DAC, the World Bank/IMF, and the UN with their specialized agencies that so far had each pursued their own respective workplans. It was quite a new experience for them to jointly develop a shared vision and common principles about fighting poverty.

Those experts were acutely aware of the need for approval by all UN member states, if any action was ever to take place. Thus, they opted for a short convincing list of goals, as little contentious as possible, focusing on the worst deprivations and based on as much robust indicators as possible. Left out were, for example, reproductive health as being too contentious, or governance as being too difficult to measure and seen as too much political interference. Civil society and NGOs were not invited to those closed doors meetings and discussions in New York. Many activist groups that were rallying against the liberalization agenda of the international financial institutions were outraged that the UN Secretary-General was teaming up with the World Bank and the IMF who were largely perceived as the enemies of poor people as they were enforcing contentious adjustment programs on many poor and middle-income countries. When learning about the draft goals, many NGOs were highly critical of them, denouncing them as too simple, too weak on donors' commitments and leaving out important issues. Nevertheless, the clarity and simplicity of the goals were catching, and the unwavering focus on fighting poverty and deprivations had never been spelled out so clearly before. And the way they were presented, without any ideological fetters or political framing about who was responsible for poverty and destitution, further added up to them being a convincing concept.

In 2001, the UN Secretary-General officially introduced with his report "Road map towards the implementation of the United Nations Millennium Declaration" this new set of eight goals: the Millennium Development Goals (MDGs). They came in an annex, each with time-bound and quantitative targets, 18 in total, and selected, measurable indicators, 48 in total. Still reluctantly and hesitantly, civil society eventually decided to jump on the bandwagon and use the new goals as much as possible for pushing for results and for regularly following-up with governments regarding their commitments (Hulme 2017: 63–67).

The MDGs were the first undertaking of the UN to use goal-setting with specific figures and numbers, quantified and time-bound targets for assessing progress in the fight against poverty and deprivations. The new goals were not about national development of nation-states, transformation of their national economies or empty national state coffers; they were about humans and their individual wellbeing. One could look into the eyes of people that were poor and suffering and that would receive the assistance provided. Development was now synonymous with eradicating poverty.

The UN and their agencies took over a leading role in steering and implementing this revived development agenda. They had managed to stay away from the political, ideological blame game of responsibilities for development and underdevelopment, and could now act as the impartial broker and hub of expertise that everyone could trust and rely on.

The MDGs were the first specific framework for development ever. As the developing countries had not been involved in the drafting, in the beginning, they were not only refusing this agenda from the rich countries but were also disappointed by their weak commitments. The only goal directed at developed countries was goal 8 (global partnership) that was in fact introduced in the end only to win the acceptance of the poor countries. Many contentious but essential issues, like trade, global finance and investment, where packed into this partnership goal that was very general and unspecific, anyway. It didn't have any timelines and lacked quantitative targets. The power play was obvious: the rich countries were ready to support the poor but were not ready to submit themselves to any deadlines or measurable criteria and, thus, possible criticism of not complying with them. But any demand for more concrete donor commitment probably would have led to the US withdrawing from the MDGs. They were one of the biggest donors that everyone wanted to keep on board. But the Bush administration was very critical about the MDGs, anyway, and was already protracting the negotiations and even threatening to stymie the whole MDG endeavor (Hulme 2007: 16; Hulme/Fukuda-Parr 2017: 67–68).

In the end, a new donor–recipient aid architecture with clearly defined roles was born: while developing countries were expected to improve their policies and governance, and implement poverty reduction strategies and programs, the developed countries were most of all expected to provide more and better aid but also open their markets and enhance trade. The specific financing agreement, reconfirming the 0.7 percent pledge of developed countries' gross national product as the financing aid target, in place already since 1970, was set up in 2002 at the Monterrey International Conference on Financing for Development (FfD). But the outcome document, that also established financing as a separate track at the UN, could only be signed with a wording leaving it open when the 0.7 target should be reached by industrialized countries (McArthur 2014: 20–21).

How much the environment was only an afterthought, if at all, illustrates the way the environmental goal was introduced into the MDGs. Mark Malloch-Brown, then the head of UNDP, recalled in an interview that the document was already on its way to the printing press, when walking along the corridor he ran into the head of the UN Environment Programme, and it suddenly crossed his mind that they had forgotten a goal about the environment. They rushed back to the office to put it in (Tran 2012).

However, the adoption of the MDGs didn't ignite immediate action in the fight against poverty. In fact, it took five years for the MDGs to really take off. As the approach of using goals and targets was new, donors, recipients, multilateral organizations, and civil society needed time to adjust their planning, programming, and reporting to the MDG framework. Considering that the MDG implementation period was set for 15 years, taking one-third of this time just for getting started and designing the necessary tools and programs, illustrates to which extent this was a break with the past and a new era of development cooperation.

Though lacking any scientific proof about how to eradicate poverty, the MDGs looked like a scientific plan. After all, the MDGs managed to condense and reduce the complex story about poverty into a simple shortlist with some very specific numbers on what to achieve. Certainly, this shortlist was incomplete and in parts an obviously random selection. But it unfolded unprecedented success in drawing global attention to the most miserable, appealing to many governments, parliaments, civil society organizations, foundations, and anyone dedicated to doing good and making the world a better place. Undoubtedly, the simplified message about eradicating poverty was much more powerful and effective than long and lofty UN declarations. And the MDGs came with the remarkable narrative that it was possible to end poverty within one generation (Awortwi/Musahara 2016: 263–264; Fukuda-Parr 2017: 120–124; Melamed/Sumner 2011: 14–15).

Naturally, the MDGs also received a lot of criticism. The voices denouncing the simplification of the development agenda and leaving out many complex aspects of poverty were numerous (Fukuda-Parr 2017: 7–8, 27–28; Smith 2010). For some they were an arbitrary and unbalanced picking of some aspects of development, woefully neglecting important issues, such as democracy, human rights, participation and empowerment, conflict and crises, trade, financial flows, governance, gender equality, environment, or the voice of developing countries in international financial institutions. Further criticism was about them being one-size-fits-all goals, neglecting the very different situations and development stages of countries and their respective national priorities. The MDGs were statistically focusing on national averages and global levels, leaving out the full picture, especially marginalized groups and people that were usually most likely elusive to those general statistics. The MDGs also didn't take into account the distinct types of poverty, if it was primarily stemming from temporary aggravating factors, like economic downturns or crop failure, or from rather structural factors, like crisis and violence, discrimination, geographic disadvantages, or systemic social exclusion. Structural and entrenched poverty could keep people for generations in destitution, making it much harder to break out of systemic cycles of deprivations. And, there was no mentioning of the heavy toll on the environment by following the example of the rich countries that fatally were still considered as a role model (Awortwi/Musahara 2016: 3, 269; Besada et al. 2017: 4–5; Fukuda-Parr 2017: 41–51, 90–92; Nayyar 2012: 10–14; Melamed/Sumner 2011: 22–23; Smith 2010; UNDESA 2014: 1–3, 8–10).

Despite all criticism, in hindsight, during the times of the MDGs the world achieved tremendous successes in the fight against poverty. Although it is difficult to say what would have happened without the MDGs, the sheer numbers are impressing:

The primary goal of globally halving the share of people living in extreme poverty was achieved. The number was reduced by more than half, from 1.9 billion people in 1990 to 836 million in 2015. By 1990[1], nearly half of all people in the developing world lived in extreme poverty, in 2015, it was 14 percent.

The proportion of chronically undernourished people fell from 23 percent in 1990 to 13 percent in 2015.

The education goal was globally met as the number of out-of-school children of primary school fell from 100 million in 2000 to 57 million in 2015. An estimated 59 million to 111 million more students had completed primary school as of 2013 compared to before 2000.

The number of people in the working middle class, living on more than $4 a day, nearly tripled between 1991 and 2015.

The proportion of women as paid workers outside the agricultural sector increased from 35 percent in 1990 to 41 percent in 2015.

The number of under-five child-deaths declined from 13 million in 1990 to 6 million in 2015.

The proportion of births assisted by skilled health personnel rose from 59 percent in 1990 to 71 percent in 2014.

New HIV infections dropped by 40 percent between 2000 and 2013. And the number of people living with HIV and receiving antiretroviral therapy rose from 800,000 in 2003 to over 13 million in 2014.

The number of people with access to an improved source of drinking water rose from 76 percent in 1990 to 91 percent in 2015.

Overall, an estimated range of 21–29.7 million lives were saved during the MDG era compared with the same period before the MDGs. This amounts to 8.8 million to 17.3 million children under the age of 5 that didn't die. Much of this can be attributed to the outstanding improvements in health, very much propelled by the specialized funds that were set up, such as The Global Fund to fight AIDS, Tuberculosis and Malaria. No issue was closer linked to the MDGs than HIV/AIDS treatment and making medication accessible to the poor. Health and education were with their sweeping successes the clear MDG champions (McArthur 2013: 160–161; McArthur/Rasmussen 2017: 42–45).

Of course, the MDGs also suffered a lot of setbacks and shortcomings: conflicts and violence remained the biggest threat to human development. By 2014, conflicts had forced almost 60 million people to flee their homes – the highest level recorded since World War II. Fragile and conflict-affected countries had the highest poverty rates. In 2015, about 800 million people still lived in extreme poverty. And each day, 16,000 children died before their fifth birthday, mostly from preventable causes. Sub-Sahara Africa remained the center of poverty and destitution, with unabated food insecurity, a rise of extreme poverty, high child and maternal mortality, and large numbers of people living in slums. Gender equality also remained a goal far from being achieved. The biggest loser during these years was the environment, as all developing countries experienced substantial environmental degradation with diminishing forests, declining clean and safe water resources, and more droughts, floods, landslides, and a changing climate. Altogether, only three and a half goals were fully achieved, while the majority of the targets was missed. While there were many near misses, there were some clear and very alarming misses which eventually leaves a mixed picture (Ritchie/Roser 2018; UNDP 2016; United Nations 2015: 4–7).

The MDGs just set benchmarks but left it to those deciding about policies and programs what exactly should be done to achieve these. Hence, this left much room for maneuver what poverty reduction and development could entail, quite diverse approaches and, of course, sometimes rather frustrating results. But it was never the intention of the authors contriving the MDGs to devise a set of ready-to-implement development strategies. This, most probably, would have been a frustrating, stillborn undertaking at the UN, given the manifold views on development policies, and the very different priorities and development stages of the developing countries. Obviously, they needed strategies tailored to their respective situation. Hence, simplification was the game, and it was tempting to just call on world leaders to "make that promise come true" (Dervis 2005), without specifying what exactly that meant.

As a side effect, the MDG framework also rose awareness of the importance of data for impartial measuring and monitoring and to track what was done and what was achieved with the provided funding. The introduction of numerical targets was a key innovation of the MDGs, leading to increased accountability throughout the development system.

When the MDGs started in 2000, statistical offices were far from ready to systematically measure and report on all indicators. With growing knowledge about data and measures, in 2005, three new targets and 12 new indicators were added, regarding, for example, biodiversity loss, access to HIV/AIDS treatment or decent work. Other targets were revised, as the employment target or reallocated, as the safe drinking water target. The overhauled MDG framework, effective January 2008, contained 8 goals, 21 targets, and 60 indicators. In fact, due to the complexities of gathering and assessing all data, and the lacking statistical capacities, it was only in 2018 possible to fully assess how much of the goals and targets of the MDGs had been achieved by 2015. Subsequently, the MDG experience triggered an enormous push for sound measuring of results of programs and projects and ensuring accountability (UNDESA 2016: 11–14; United Nations 2015: 10–13).

Looking back in hindsight, were the MDGs the gamechanger in the fight against poverty? Yes and no. Given the myriads of factors that determine development paths, it is impossible to ascribe those stunning development results exclusively to the existence of the MDG framework. Many developing countries were already making steady development progress before the MDGs, and they continued at a generally consistent rate during the MDG era. China alone reduced poverty by 600 million in three decades. Vietnam had reduced poverty from 51 percent in 1990 to 14 percent in 2002. By 2005, East Asia had already achieved the poverty MDG, and South Asia was broadly on track (Fukuda-Parr 2017: 33; IBRD 2005: 2; McArthur 2013: 158–159; UNDESA 2016: 144).

And yet, the MDGs became a historic milestone in the fight against poverty, a revolution-like watershed moment of the development agenda. They were the new consensus on what development should aim at and the new reference point for assessing, comparing, and evaluating development cooperation. They were the standard for progress or setbacks, and they were the rallying cry going out into the world. They stood for development cooperation in the 21st century, and easily galvanized support throughout the UN system, with governments, civil society, and also celebrities rallying behind the goals. The fact that development assistance from developed countries increased by 66 percent between 2000 and 2014, reaching $135.2 billion, corroborated their rather unique leverage and attraction. “To say that the MDGs have been central to the last 15 years of development practice is an understatement. The defining feature of post-2000 international development policy and practice is the MDGs” (Besada et al. 2017: 5). The MDG agenda was one of the best concepts ever brought to live in the framework of the UN, easy to understand, undisputed, appealing to everyone, mustering global forces, and resources for an intrinsically good cause and apparently producing winners only. They had proven to be one of the most powerful communication tools the United Nations ever had (Luna/Montano 2017: 54–55). Such a success story, of course, had to be continued, in particular as the fight against poverty was far from over.

However, when discussing what should follow the MDGs, the elephant in the room was the relationship between development and the environment and a supposed trade-off between the two. No one wanted to question or criticize ways out of poverty, in particular the impressive success stories of many middle-income countries. However, there was also an undeniable downside. Slashing the number of people living in poverty and swelling the number of middle-class consumers was wreaking a heavy toll on the environment. This was most dramatically illustrated by the abysmal air quality in many relatively new megacities, polluted rivers or sprouting dumpsites for all sorts of trash, in particular plastic but also hazard waste. Development trajectories following the traditional Western industrialization model would inevitably lead to environmental degradation at a new frightening scale. The long-term hope and goal of the international community that poor countries someday would eradicate the scourge of poverty and poor people would enjoy opportunities and prosperity the same way people in the rich countries had been doing for many years, suddenly appeared as a daunting vision. From an environmental perspective, the inherently good and desirable goal of lifting people out of poverty had unfolded a disturbing aftertaste. Hence, in Rio 2012, merging the environmental and the development agenda for the benefit of both and to advance toward a new path of sustainable development, was perceived as the chance to possibly have it both, further progress in the fight against poverty while protecting the environment.

Note

1 The MDGs used 1990 as the reference line. The MDGs were monitoring progress by comparing the 2015 data with the data from 1990.

References

Awortwi, Nicholas/Herman Musahara (2016): *Implementation of the Millennium Development Goals: Progresses and Challenges in Some African Countries*, Oxford: African Books Collective, Project MUSE.

Barca, Stefania (2011): Energy, Property, and the Industrial Revolution Narrative. *Ecological Economics*, Vol. 70, No. 7, 15 May 2011: 1309–1315.

Besada, Hany/Leah McMillan Polonenko/Manmohan Agarwal (2017): *Did the Millennium Development Goals Work? Meeting Future Challenges with Past Lessons*, Bristol University Press, Policy Press.

Bigg, Tom (2012): Five Things We've Learnt from Rio+20, International Institute for Environment and Development. https://www.iied.org/five-things-we-ve-learnt-rio20

Caballero, Paula/Patti Londoño (2022): *Redefining Development. The Extraordinary Genesis of the Sustainable Development Goals*, Boulder/London: Lynne Rienner Publishers.

Caradonna, Jeremy L. (2014): *Sustainability. A History*, Oxford: Oxford University Press.

Carson, Rachel (1962): *Silent Spring*, Boston/New York: Penguin Twentieth-Century Classics.

Charbonnier, Pierre (2021): *Affluence and Freedom: An Environmental History of Political Ideas*, Cambridge: Polity Press.

Commission on Growth and Development (2008): *The Growth Report. Strategies for Sustained Growth and Inclusive Development*, Washington, DC: The International Bank for Reconstruction and Development/The World Bank.

Dervis, Kermal (2005): Why the Millennium Development Goals Matter, *International Herald Tribune* (European Edition), 14 September 2005.

Du Pisani, Jacobus (2006): Sustainable Development – Historical Roots of the Concept. *Environmental Sciences*, Vol. 3, No. 2, pp. 83–96.

Founex Report on Development and Environment, Carnegie Endowment for International Peace, 1971.

Fukuda-Parr, Sakiko (2017): *Millennium Development Goals. Ideas, Interests and Influence*, London/New York: Routledge.

Grober, Ulrich (2007): Deep Roots – A Conceptual History of 'Sustainable Development' (Nachhaltigkeit), Wissenschaftszentrum Berlin für Sozialforschung (WZB), February 2007.

Hardin, Garrett (1968): The Tragedy of the Commons: The Population Problem Has No Technical Solution; It Requires a Fundamental Extension in Morality. *Science*, Vol. 162, No. 3859, September 13, 1968, pp. 1243–1248.

Hulme, David (2007): The Making of the Millennium Development Goals: Human Development Meets Results-based Management in an Imperfect World, Brooks World Poverty Institute, BWPI Working Paper 16, Manchester.

Hulme, David/Sakiko Fukuda-Parr (2017): The Emergence and Spread of the Global Poverty Norm, in: Sakiko Fukuda-Parr (Ed.): *Millennium Development Goals. Ideas, Interests and Influence*, London/New York: Routledge, pp. 57–80.

IBRD – International Bank for Reconstruction and Development/The World Bank (2005): Global Monitoring Report, Millennium Development Goals: From Consensus to Momentum, Washington.

Kjørven, Olav (2016): The Unlikely Journey to the 2030 Agenda for Sustainable Development, IMPAKTER Essay, December 8, 2016. https://impakter.com/impakter-essay-unlikely-journey-2030-agenda-sustainable-development/

Little, Paul E. (1995): Ritual, Power and Ethnography at the Rio earth Summit. *Critique of Anthropology*, Vol. 15, No. 3, pp. 265–288.

Lucatello, Simone (2017): Environmental Sustainability in the 2030 Agenda: Is Mexico Up to the Task?, in: Rebecka Villanueva Ulfgard (Ed.): *Mexico and the Post-2015 Development Agenda: Contributions and Challenges*, New York: Springer Nature, pp. 195–215.

Luna, Sara/Jorge Montaño (2017): From MDGs to SDGs: A Transformative 2030 Agenda for Sustainable Development, in: Rebecka Villanueva Ulfgard (Ed.): *Mexico and the Post-2015 Development Agenda: Contributions and Challenges*, New York, pp. 53–65.

Mahathir bin Mohamed, Datuk Seri (1999): The Green Flag of Eco-imperialism. *New Perspectives Quarterly*, Vol. 6, No. 2, April 1999, pp. 8–9. https://doi.org/10.1111/0893-7850.00214

McArthur, John W. (2013): Own the Goals: What the Millennium Development Goals Have Accomplished. *Foreign Affairs*, Vol. 92, No. 2, pp. 152–162.

McArthur, John W. (2014): The Origins of the Millennium Development Goals. *The SAIS Review of International Affairs*, Vol. 34, No. 2, pp. 5–24.

McArthur, John W./Krista Rasmussen (2017): Change of Pace, Accelerations and Advances during the Millennium Development Goal Era, Global Economy & Development at the Brookings Institution, Working Paper 98, January 2017.

McNeill, John Robert/Peter Engelke (2014): *The Great Acceleration, an Environmental History of the Anthropocene since 1945*, Cambridge: Harvard University.

Melamed, Claire/Andy Sumner (2011): A Post-2015 Global Development Agreement: Why, What, Who? ODI/UNDP Cairo Workshop, 26–27 October 2011.

Millennium Ecosystem Assessment - MEA (2001–2006): Millennium Assessment Reports. https://www.millenniumassessment.org/en/index.html

Nayyar, Deepak (2012): The MDGs after 2015: Some Reflections on the Possibilities, UN System Task Team on the Post-2015 UN Development Agenda, April 2012.

OECD (1996): *Shaping the 21st Century: The Contribution of Development Co-operation, Best Practices in Development Co-operation*, Paris: OECD Publishing.

Palmer, Geoffrey (1992): The Earth Summit: What Went Wrong At Rio? *Washington University Law Quarterly*, Vol. 70, No. 4, pp. 1005–1028.

Ritchie, Hannah/Max Roser (2018): Now It Is Possible to Take Stock – Did the World Achieve the Millennium Development Goals? Published online at OurWorldInData.org. Retrieved from: https://ourworldindata.org/millennium-development-goals [Online Resource]

Sanwal, Mukul (2015): *The World's Search for Sustainable Development, a Perspective from the Global South*, Cambridge: Cambridge University Press.

Smil, Vaclav (2017): *Energy and Civilization: A History*, Cambridge, MA: Massachusetts Institute of Technology.

Smith, Dan (2010): So What's Wrong with the MDGs? Dan Smith's blog, September 20, 2010. https://dansmithsblog.com/2010/09/20/so-whats-wrong-with-the-mdgs/

Strong, Maurice (1992): The 1992 Earth Summit: An Inside View. https://www.mauricestrong.net/index.php?option=com_content&view=article&id=206&Itemid=104

Tran, Mark (2012): Mark Malloch-Brown: Developing the MDGs Was a Bit Like Nuclear Fusion. *The Guardian*, November 16, 2012. https://www.theguardian.com/global-development/2012/nov/16/mark-malloch-brown-mdgs-nuclear

UNDESA (2014): TST Issues Briefs, a Compendium of Issues Briefs Prepared by the United Nations Inter-Agency Technical Support Team for the United Nations General Assembly Open Working Group on Sustainable Development Goals, New York.

UNDESA (2016): Learning from National Policies Supporting MDG Implementation, E/2015/50/Rev.1, ST/ESA/360, New York.

UNDP (2016): From the MDGs to Sustainable Development for All, Lessons from 10 Years of Practice, New York.

United Nations (1973): Report of the United Nations Conference on the Human Environment, Stockholm, 5–16 June 1972, New York.

United Nations (2015): The Millennium Development Goals Report 2015, New York.

World Commission on Environment and Development (1987): Our Common Future, from One Earth to One World. https://sustainabledevelopment.un.org/content/documents/5987our-common-future.pdf

3

SETTING OUT ON THE BUMPY ROAD TO THE SDGs

Going sustainable ushers in a plan for the whole world

Setting the scene at the UN: Deep learning about what exactly is sustainable development

After the Rio summit decision in 2012 to merge the poverty and environmental agenda and to bring together the three dimensions of sustainable development, social, economic, and environmental, the aftermath was bustling with analyzing and discussing options for post-2015. The UN initiated numerous reports and a comprehensive stocktaking about what the Millennium Development Goals (MDGs) had achieved and where they lagged behind, what had worked and what not and which conclusions should be drawn for a successor agenda. The by-far biggest and comprehensive exercise in this regard was a 27-member "UN High-Level Panel of Eminent Persons on the post-2015 Development Agenda" that should draft recommendations for a new global development framework. The High-Level Panel was co-chaired by former President of Indonesia Susilo Bambang Yudhoyono, President Ellen Johnson Sirleaf of Liberia, and Prime Minister David Cameron of the United Kingdom, representing a middle-income, a developing and a developed country.

Some of the developing countries were, in fact, rather suspicious of this High-Level Panel as it reminded them of the closed circle of development experts that had once cooked up the MDGs in backroom meetings. But this time, everything was supposed to be very different. The High-Level Panel with the support of the UN system started a remarkable outreach process literally trying to cover almost everyone and everything under the sun. The UN launched the platform "The World We Want"[1] to support and complement the High-Level Panel's work. It consulted a massive swathe of people, including over 5000 civil society organizations, from about 120 countries. A UN-initiated global survey, "My World 2015,"[2] asked people to list six challenges they faced in

DOI: 10.4324/9781032702681-3

their lives and what governments should do for a better world. It was an unprecedented consultation in terms of the number and the diversity of people weighing in, more than 10 million in the end (Ladd 2016: 32–34). And over 100 additional national consultations and 11 thematic consultations, subsequently, produced two more reports: "The Global Conversation Begins"[3] (March 2013) and "A Million Voices: The World We Want"[4] (September 2013).

For the High-Level Panel, it was impossible to take up all the reflections and ideas, but it was equally impossible to ignore them. This vast global process was, in fact, driven by a new understanding that development policy should be an open and inclusive process that could only truly benefit people, if people from all walks of life, in particular from developing countries, were given an opportunity to weigh in. As hunger and the most severe deprivations were still afflicting many people, it was no surprise that many deemed fighting poverty, education and health as essential top priorities for the future agenda. But interestingly, issues, such as honest and responsive government, protection against crime and violence or protecting forests, rivers, and oceans, were considered as almost equally important. Many participants wished them to be part of the new agenda (Ladd 2016: 24). The final report of the Panel, issued in May 2013, "A New Global Partnership: Eradicate Poverty and Transform Economies through Sustainable Development"[5] eventually drafted 12 goals with complementary targets as an input into the post-2015 process.

In the meantime, UN member states had started the preparations for the official post-2015 negotiations. Macharia Kamau from Kenya and Csaba Körösi from Hungary were appointed as co-chairs of the Open Working Group (OWG) and had to organize the process. At the UN, large and complex processes and negotiations are usually led by two co-chairs, one from the Global South and one from the Global North. This is to broaden confidence in the process by all parties with no regional grouping dominating, and possibly ease compromise and a by all sides accepted result. At Rio, member states had limited the OWG seats to only 30 participants to keep the discussions manageable and focused. Although no one really knew what to expect from this upcoming OWG, everyone wanted to take part in this new game in town. Eventually, 70 member states had expressed their desire to participate. To not exclude or alienate anyone who wanted to engage, it took painful seven months to eventually agree on sharing most seats by two or three countries. This meant seatmates had to draft a joint statement to be delivered during the discussions. This run on the OWG seats revealed the fear of many member states of missing out on potential major decisions determining the future agenda to come. And they should be proven right.

How important a transparent, open, inclusive and consensus-oriented process is, had been demonstrated by the failure of the Copenhagen Climate Conference in 2009. Secret work behind closed doors, a secret host-country text, and the announcement of an agreement that most delegations were unaware of had led to a deep, lingering distrust between developed and developing countries. This was the example that no one wanted to repeat.

But what happened next was pretty much the opposite of Copenhagen and something unheard of before at the United Nations. Being aware of the fear of yet another secret process and the limited knowledge about the various very specialized fields of sustainable development, the two co-chairs decided to take the time for some deep learning for all delegations. Numerous experts and practitioners should contribute to fostering a thorough understanding of the interlinkages between poverty and the environment, between poor people turning into middle-class consumers and the subsequent ecological footprint, between enhancing agricultural output and harming biodiversity, or the role of equality, gender, good governance and effective institutions in fighting poverty and protecting the environment. In contrast to usual UN business, NGOs, UN agencies, and other organizations were invited to this deep learning. By giving all stakeholders, including the private sector and civil society, the chance to weigh in, the co-chairs wanted to foster a stronger commitment by all to the new agenda. Many governments were initially profoundly uncomfortable with this approach and would have preferred a strictly intergovernmental process. But with time, this new open-door and open-mic approach was embraced by all (Caballero/Londoño 2022: 72).

Another objective of this stocktaking phase was also to depoliticize the different topics. Usually, at the UN exactly the opposite is happening: topics are being politicized, and countries argue along the often ideologically and historically grown blocs for or against an issue. Discussions on development topics for decades have been shaped by a North–South dividing line. Usually, this polarizing North–South dynamic, often incriminatory by nature and with donors versus recipients and vice versa, fails to reflect the complexity and reality of many topics. And unsurprisingly, these discussions are of limited value and rarely produce concrete results (Chasek et al. 2016). Thus, when setting up the OWG, Colombia had fought for taking out politics to avoid exactly these types of debates that often woefully miss out on agreeing on meaningful action. The seat-sharing exercise already considerably contributed to loosening the rigid bloc structure as seatmates could deliver only one statement. In particular for some rather unusual seatmates, like Bangladesh, Korea, Saudi Arabia or Iran, Japan, and Nepal, this had ushered in some unexpected convergence processes (Kamau et al. 2018: 96–99). In addition, many issues, in fact, turned out to be so new, complex, double-edged, interlinked and of global relevance that many countries were not quite sure, where a North–South dividing line was, if at all. In the first place, everyone wanted to thoroughly understand what exactly was at stake and, of course, where and how exactly countries could potentially win or lose. In some cases, it was rather interesting to witness how some of the most diametrically opposed and politically charged relationships mellowed over the eight sessions (Chasek et al. 2016).

Another equally important objective of the stocktaking was to reconcile and bring together the so-called "two parallel universes" (Kamau et al. 2018: 99) or the "two rather entrenched communities, with largely separate worldviews" (Kjørven 2016): the poverty agenda and the environmental agenda. Both the poverty and the environmental community were anxious that their respective agendas might be watered down, that they would be losing support, attention and, most importantly, funding to the respective other crowd. The developed countries were wary that environmental action might lose focus and impact due to too many countries claiming exemptions and flexible regulations because of their development status. And the developing countries were wary that their development might be slowed down or hampered due to ambitious environmental standards. Thus, the big question was if despite all differences in political priorities and development stages both rich and poor countries would be willing to agree on one agenda and eventually apply the same goals and targets (Dodds et al. 2017: 17–18). In addition, there was much to learn about how to meaningfully integrate the economic dimension that so far had been rather seen as an alien actor with a different agenda. Balancing development and environment, weighing the benefits from growth and the harmful impacts on the environment while identifying an acceptable way of setting out to sustainable development for all turned out to be extremely difficult.

Some examples illustrate the main quarrels and controversies, often cutting across traditional dividing lines and negotiation patterns:

Debating a possible goal on energy meant to venture out into the uncharted territory of renewable energies, new technologies, and new infrastructure that were still being developed and, in addition, were much more expensive. The oil-exporting countries, in particular Saudi Arabia, and those relying on fossil fuels were advocating for cheap energy as this was vital for many poor people to leave behind poverty. Many European countries, however, were strongly advocating for clean and green energy and a goal on climate change. Developing countries were wary of the EU's firm interest in a strong climate commitment, provoking suspicion and fear that this would lead to curtailing their economic development. And the EU was concerned that, without engagement by the developing countries, in particular the middle-income countries, most efforts to curb climate degradation would by far fall short of the required global impact. However, some developing countries, like the Small Island Developing States (SIDS) group, vividly joined the call for halting climate change and reducing dependency on fossil fuels. The devastating repercussions of climate change on their countries and rising sea levels, in fact, made their survival dependent on reducing carbon emissions and transitioning toward renewable energies. Other countries like the US, Australia, and Canada feared that the energy debate would be linked with the contentious climate negotiations which they wanted to avoid.

The compromise eventually was to have one target on ensuring universal access to energy, without specifying what kind of energy, one target on increasing renewable energy and one target on increasing energy efficiency. Like this, every party would be satisfied, and fossil fuels were simply not mentioned, so nothing was excluded or banned. Regarding the contentious fossil fuel subsidies, the compromise eventually was a rather awkward and cumbersome target, advocating to "rationalize inefficient fossil fuel subsidies." Tellingly, this was not put under the energy goal but under the goal on sustainable consumption and production.

Regarding the climate topic, the post-2015 process had to define its relationship with the climate track. As the climate negotiations, that would eventually conclude in the Paris Agreement, were taking place in parallel, the OWG eventually opted to acknowledge in the draft climate goal that the United Nations Framework Convention on Climate Change (UNFCCC) was the primary forum for negotiating the global response to climate change. This meant there was at least one contentious issue where the OWG had decided to leave the details for another setting.

Regarding economic growth, the developing countries were strongly advocating for a stand-alone goal as growth was a precondition for ending poverty. Many developed countries, however, were rather reluctant about this proposal as in their view this would cement old-fashioned growth models. Eventually, a common ground could be identified by adding targets on employment, decoupling economic growth from environmental degradation, and shifting toward more sustainable lifestyles. But the dominating mantra of growth that developing countries insisted on being a primary issue remained a linchpin.

The discussion about infrastructure and industrialization was reflecting the same patterns. The Western countries were reluctant about a goal on industrialization as lacking the necessary future-oriented vision for a sustainable development agenda. But developing countries argued that the developed countries had grown rich through industrialization, so they insisted on their right to taking the same chance. In particular, the African Group was very outspoken about the need for industrialization and infrastructure. Again, adding targets on employment and an increase in resource-efficiency and clean and environmentally sound industrial processes was the compromise for a draft goal.

Inequality was one of the rather new topics in the OWG with the developing countries passionately advocating for a stand-alone goal on this issue. Their input was further corroborated by some astounding inputs from economist and Nobel Laureate Joseph Stiglitz, Oxfam, and other NGOs, about rising and deeply troubling inequalities in rich countries. Inequality started claiming attention as the underrated and overlooked universal topic, haunting both developed and developing countries. The developed countries, however, were rather critical of a stand-alone goal and favored a reference to reducing inequalities between social groups in the poverty goal. While the latter proposal was perceived by developing countries as a meddling into their own economic and social fabric, the developed countries perceived a new inequality goal as an opener for tallying up historical grievances about colonialism, exploitation, and potential compensation (Kamau et al. 2018: 92–96). Eventually, the compromise for a draft goal was to include both, inequality within and among countries in a new stand-alone goal. Besides an enhanced representation of developing countries in international economic and financial institutions, it also stressed equal opportunities for all people through legislation, representation, and policies.

Discussing sustainable consumption and production was another new topic and concurrently an eye-opener on how much the world was intertwined. Scientific research in this field had shown how much the Western lifestyle was unsustainable in many ways, and how much consumption and production patterns were globally impacting economies, trade, and the ecological footprint. Again, like during the Rio negotiations, proposing a wording about curtailing the lifestyles of those living in prosperity would have been difficult to adopt for all sides. After all, reaching exactly this unsustainable lifestyle was still the dream of many people in developing countries, aspiring to leave behind poverty. In the end, the draft goal contained some important targets about natural resources and waste, and also a reference to companies reporting about their performance in sustainability. But it was rather soft and weak in its language and missed quantifiable targets about waste reduction or efficient natural resource use.

Among the thorniest and most contentious discussions were those leading to goal 16, about "just, peaceful and inclusive societies." Human rights, democracy, governance, and the rule of law are controversial issues at the UN, anyway, and often fought along the lines of the traditional North–South divide. Some developing countries didn't want to include a goal on these issues at all, arguing that these wouldn't belong to a development agenda. Pakistan, India, and Sri Lanka argued that the OWG was not the right place to discuss conflict and post-conflict issues as the UN had other bodies better suited, such as the UN Security Council.[6] Others felt one goal was not enough for these important topics. Sweden, for example, was calling for two separate goals, one on freedom from violence and another on good governance and the rule of law.[7] Again others, like India, were arguing that peace was the result of development but not a precondition for it. India, China, and Brazil underscored vociferously that there was no internationally agreed definition of the rule of law, only a so-called Western definition which they rejected. For much of the debate chances were high that in the end there would be no goal on any of these issues.

Interestingly, the decisive sway came from several smaller countries, like Sierra Leone, Timor Leste, or Liberia, the "g7+ Group of Conflict-affected and Fragile States." They had only recently emerged from violent conflicts and perfectly knew what they were talking about when advocating for peace and good governance. Timor Leste, for example, dramatically underscored "the lived experience that there can be no development without peace, and there can be no peace without development." As long as conflict, insecurity, and violence dominated, all financial investments would be to no avail and in fact would be wasted.[8] During the MDG era, a lot of evidence was clearly showing that violence, conflict, a lack of rule of law, and weak institutions were the main reasons for lack of development progress and missing on many MDGs. Conflict and crisis actually meant development in reverse, as some long-term studies had shown: the average cost of civil war was equivalent to more than 30 years of GDP growth for a medium-sized developing country; thus, it took 30 years to recover and reach the status quo ante before the war. For trade it took about 20 years to recover. And the drivers of conflict and violence were many: socio-economic inequalities, lack of jobs and welfare systems, human rights violations and abuses, exclusion of groups or parts of society, or disputes over land, resources or possession. Thus, preventing violent conflicts was the best investment in development and an indispensable basis for development to bear fruit in the first place (UNDESA 2014: 225–229; United Nations/World Bank 2018).

Eventually, the g7+ post-conflict countries, as the living proof of the toll of conflict, were most outspoken about including a goal related to governance and peace. They were pushing relentlessly and convincingly colleagues from other developing countries that ending violence and conflict was crucial and eventually managed to melt down the opposition from key developing countries. However, goal 16 about peaceful and inclusive societies, in fact, made it to the OWG draft only due to some additional horse-trading by not mentioning the rule of law in the title and in exchange for some points in the goals on inequality, industrialization, and sustainable consumption and production (Kamau et al. 2018: 202–203).

Finally, there was a telling debate about the relationship between fighting poverty and protecting the environment and about the increasingly complex question of responsibilities. The emerging economies or middle-income countries were in an unusual, sometimes uncomfortable position, struggling with both the problems of the developed and the developing world. On the one hand, due to economic development on the fast lane, they were feeling the heat from mounting environmental degradation that needed to be curbed. But on the other hand, they wanted to keep up the momentum and their high growth rates to further expand prosperity and wellbeing. Deflecting from the obvious environmental toll and shortcomings in their own countries, they were instead demanding more action from developed countries. Addressing the rich countries, the Indian Ambassador said those "who rushed toward development without much regard for the needs of the global environment" should be the ones shouldering the burden of cleaning up and paying for the cleaning up.[9] Despite having turned into middle-income countries, they were rather unconvincingly refusing to take over more financial or other forms of commitment. However, the already blurred dividing line between perpetrators and victims was relentlessly further vanishing. It was obvious that a growing number of developing countries had turned into perpetrators themselves and that every country was at least responsible for domestic legislation, oversight and cleaning up in one's own backyard. Obviously, the enticing but flawed belief in growing first and cleaning up later was still very much alive.

During the months of debating the future goals and targets in the OWG, most participants went through positive feelings of getting a deeper understanding of the complex issues at stake but also feelings of overwhelming confusion and drowning in scientific and technological depths. Another important takeaway for everyone was to acknowledge that there was still a long way to go for science to fully understand the human impact on the earth, and for research and innovation to produce sustainable solutions for all aspects of life.

Eventually, the delegations came to the point where they had to decide about how many goals and targets the new agenda should comprise. They were looking for something that was catchy, understandable and communicable, but at the same time neither too simplified and superficial, nor too complex and overwhelmingly detailed. And, of course, it had to be manageable. Having all of this, appeared like squaring the circle. The eight MDG goals had proven to be a comprehensive but still communicable agenda. Hence, some favored sticking to the number of eight goals and simply adjust and broaden the content. Others were advocating for 10 or 12 goals as a good number for easy messaging. Regarding the targets, the numbers were floating between 30 for the whole agenda, and a maximum number of eight under each goal which would have landed at somewhere over 100 targets. The final proposal by the co-chairs in their zero-draft eventually comprised 17 goals and 212 targets.

The question about the right number of goals and targets was also linked to finding the right balance between the three dimensions of sustainable development that the agenda should address: economic, social, and environmental. During the Rio negotiations, having a powerful environmental commitment at the expense of the fight against poverty was one of the major fears of the developing countries. The African Group was particularly concerned that attention and resources would be drawn away from eradicating poverty, and the poor would be even more left behind by this new agenda.[10] There was an undeniable tension between on the one hand drafting an ambitious visionary agenda, tackling all critical challenges for human action to remain within planetary boundaries. On the other hand, the unfinished business of eradicating poverty had to remain of primary importance.

After more than 18 months of intense deliberations and discussions in 13 sessions, debating over 58 agenda items, presentations by more than 80 experts, deep diving into all possible topics that could play a role in defining the future sustainability agenda and tossing back and forth all sorts of arguments, in July 2014, the OWG agreed on its final proposal of 17 goals and 169 targets. The General Assembly adopted this OWG report in September as the basis for the subsequent intergovernmental negotiations.

With the closing of the OWG, the most unlikely and unusual experiment at the UN came to an end. It had started with very mixed feelings, with a lot of skepticism and doubts as well as enthusiasm and confidence, and ended in a surprisingly comprehensive and balanced draft. In hindsight, it looked like a marvelous miracle "that the interests of 193 UN Member States and widespread stakeholder input had been narrowed down into 17 goals…" (Chasek et al. 2016). And the OWG had achieved even more. The whole process had dramatically and unequivocally laid bare the complexity and interconnectedness of current social, economic, and environmental challenges. An unprecedented sense of unity was spawn, bringing all countries together in the firm resolve to tackle the sustainability challenges jointly and comprehensively. It was the first time, all UN member countries had collectively conceded that in all countries things were going wrong, and that change and transformation was dearly needed all over the world. It was not any more about one group of better-off countries supposed to lead the way and the others supposed to follow them, it was about the whole world that had to change course in a fundamental and thorough way.

But, the idea by Colombia of taking out politics through not following the UN rules with the OWG, had only worked to a certain extent. True, the setup had loosened the formalized and politicized UN world for a couple of months. It had allowed some unusually frank debating and open-minded learning, pondering, and exchanging of arguments that many certainly would appreciate having more often at the UN. Yet, all participants were aware that despite this being a most welcome and valuable experience, it was only temporary. A return to the official UN procedures, including an official adoption of the final agenda was indispensable. Much of the politicized incriminatory arguing back and forth was clearly toned down and subdued, but eventually started bouncing back when it came down to agreeing on the single goals and targets for the final draft. And with this everyone was supposed to get back to the usual UN business.

Bringing the SDGs into this world: A hodgepodge of politics, civil society, science, and many vested interests

When the official negotiations were about to start, there was a lot of uncertainty what should and could happen in the following months. Most topics and controversies had already been debated and churned through by all delegations, sensitive compromises had already been forged and grudgingly accepted. And each party knew about the strengths and weaknesses of the OWG proposal and had eventually agreed to it. With a view to the now formally starting negotiations, the big question was to which extent this draft of goals and targets should be reopened and formally negotiated. The sensitivities were quite high as a lot of time and energy had already been spent on the OWG draft. Many developing countries were quite satisfied with the text and rather worried that opening up the draft would lead to diluting and watering down some crucial points. They feared eventually ending up on a slippery slope to painstakingly renegotiating all goals and targets. The US, Canada, Japan, and many Europeans, however, were less satisfied with the OWG draft and were willing to reopen the text with the hope of lifting the bar higher and tweaking some of the goals and targets. They had the feeling there was too much compromise and too little ambition in the OWG draft which would fall short of igniting the transformation needed for a sustainable world (Donoghue 2020).

Against this backdrop, it was clear that any possible redrafting could only be done with utmost caution to not jeopardize the entire very delicate OWG set. In addition, the time constraints were extremely tight as the 2030 Agenda was supposed to be adopted in September 2015 which meant the final draft had to be finished by summer. There was effectively only half a year for the negotiations to produce a final text. Nevertheless, the co-chairs for the negotiations, Macharia Kamau from Kenya, who had already co-chaired the OWG, and David Donoghue from Ireland, took the chance to carefully nudge delegations to work for an ambitious result. Being aware of the shortcomings of the OWG draft and concurrently seeing the opportunity to reach an agenda that would ignite transformative change in real life, they maneuvered delegations to cautiously opening up the goals and targets where necessary and engage constructively.

The official negotiations, starting in January 2015, had a very different dynamic compared to the OWG. As they now followed the formal UN setup and processes, there was no seat sharing any more, only the traditional regional blocs along the North–South divide instead. Usually, the G77 and China[11] deliver a position on behalf of the developing countries, and the Western countries, such as the EU members, the US, Canada, or Japan, articulate the position of the developed countries. Some smaller coalitions, such as the African Group, the Arab Group, the Group of the Least-Developed Countries (LDCs), or the SIDS weigh in on specific issues important to them, but are rarely a game-changer. The Secretary-General isn't a party in intergovernmental negotiations, but can support, persuade, argue in favor or against, propel discussions on certain topics and rally opinion around certain issues.

There were some initial anxieties that with the official negotiations the whole process would eventually be bogged down in tedious UN bloc-to-bloc confrontations, ripping apart the OWG draft. But gladly, the broad support and enthusiasm for the SDGs that had been created and nurtured during the OWG sessions was still lingering in the meeting rooms. Unlike the painful and confrontational Rio+20 negotiations, delegations had much more a common understanding of working on a joint endeavor that now needed to be brought across the finish line. The still tangible very special OWG atmosphere helped to keep the usual tit-for-tat or bloc-to-bloc dynamics at bay – at least for some time.

One interesting suggestion by the co-chairs, supported by the UN Secretary-General in his synthesis report from December 2014, was to undertake a "technical review" of the OWG draft, in particular the proposed indicators for operationalizing the SDGs (United Nations 2014). The aim of such a review, so the rationale of the co-chairs, was to ensure that all indicators underpinning the goals and targets would be fully measurable, achievable, and consistent with existing standards, agreements, and the latest technical thinking and scientific evidence. The indicators were not part of the official negotiations, as these were usually considered a technical issue and, thus, developed by the UN Statistical Commission. However, in this politically highly sensitive environment, the dividing line between technical and political decisions was rather blurred. After having concluded on an OWG draft with many sensitive and difficult compromises, member states were extremely cautious that these compromises wouldn't be opened up by declaring something as an ostensibly technical matter. Both member states and the UN Statistical Commission, working on suggestions for such a technical revision, were afraid of ending up arguing less about the substance but arguing more about what would be a political and what a technical decision (Dodds et al. 2017: 81). As a result, a new group was established in 2015, an Interagency and Expert Group on Sustainable Development Goal Indicators (IAEG-SDGs), that will be dealt with in the next chapter.

Many delegations acknowledged that during the OWG drafting there hadn't been enough time to produce sound targets for all goals. Hence, some of them were rather vague or incomplete to the extent with a few still containing "x" as a measure that had to be filled with content yet. Eventually, the co-facilitators made 19 proposals for target revisions of which, after overcoming resistance by the G77 regarding any amendment, 12 found the way into the final document. Throughout the whole targets and indicators' discussions, the co-chairs skillfully used the word "tweak" to imply that changes would only be minor and of a rather technical nature to allay any suspicion that the delicate political balances and comprises would be overturned.

The goals and targets were supposed to be the core part of the new agenda, embedded in a frame consisting of a declaration, the means of implementation and the global partnership, as well as a follow-up and review process. Altogether this should form the 2030 Agenda for Sustainable Development.

The declaration of the 2030 Agenda, laying out the purpose, scope, and commitment of the agenda and the underlying principles and tenets, turned out to be quite a tedious issue. Most delegations specifically saw the declaration as the opportunity to break away from the usual UN speak and "communicate clearly the core messages at the heart of the post-2015 development agenda and serve as an inspiring call to action" (Dodds et al. 2017: 79). However, communicating this new agenda was easier said than done. The SDGs, 17 in numbers and some of them rather unwieldy, provoked doubts about how they could be implemented successfully, if people didn't understand what this complex agenda was about. The convincing power and charm of the MDGs had been their simplicity and clarity. They were a compelling and clear list of the major destitutions that needed to be addressed to fight poverty. The SDGs, however, were lacking this charm of having simple and clear messages as they were of a much more complex nature and spanning many more topics. The important question of communicating and promoting the new agenda raised considerable concerns. Some delegations were deeply worried, if the supposed transformation would ever happen, as the gist of this new agenda was not that clear-cut and focused. The Dutch delegate, for example, underscored the need to draft a catchy, cogent, and convincing appeal to the world that "is understood by all beyond the square mile around the UN premises here in New York." Hence, the task was "to cast complex issues in simple, understandable language," so the delegate from the Netherlands who hoped that even his 13-year old daughter would understand the message and could relate to it (Kamau et al. 2018: 225–226).

While every delegation was aware of the communication challenge, every delegation was likewise concerned that their specific issues would not be sacrificed for the sake of catchy messages. In the end, it had to be a compromise between what was politically wanted and agreeable at the UN but still communicable, and what was scientifically imperative for a real sustainability agenda. The heated debates eventually produced some catchy communication ideas, such as to use the "five Ps" as a slogan or communication tool to convey the key contents of the agenda: people, planet, prosperity, peace, and partnership. Defining "leaving no one behind" as a principle of the agenda, to the surprise of the co-chairs didn't meet any resistance and would later become a popular short title (Donoghue 2020).

The declaration also served as the fallback option for some issues that were too contentious or too broad to be linked to specific goals and targets. This happened, for example, with human rights that, as usual, caused vitriolic debates. From the beginning of the post-2015 process, this issue had stirred much controversy between those delegations, mostly from the Global North, adamant about granting them a principal status and possibly even a stand-alone goal, and those delegations, mostly from the Global South, opposing anything that would go beyond already agreed language. During last-minute debates, African and Arab states were seeking to weaken language on human rights and also gender equality. Eventually human rights were just reconfirmed in the declaration, mentioned in only one goal, rather surprisingly in the goal on education, and in the means of implementation.

Another difficult topic was the monitoring and follow-up mechanism. As the OWG hadn't managed to present a useful proposal on the question of establishing a robust system for monitoring and reviewing, delegations had to resolve this during the negotiations. In the MDG era, the UN had accompanied their implementation mainly with data collection, monitoring and projections, as much as it was possible at the time. But there was no mechanism to effectively push or urge member states to live up to their commitments, if they failed them. At the Rio+20 summit, member states had decided to establish a new forum, the High-Level Political Forum (HLPF). It was launched in 2013 to ensure the follow-up of the SDGs during their 15 years of implementation. It was supposed to give guidance and produce recommendations, improve cooperation and coordination as well as promote transparency and participation. When debating how to flesh out the HLPF to turn it into an effective follow-up mechanism, most delegations were torn between on the one hand wanting to ensure that reviewing and reporting progress or lack of thereof would be done based on scientific evidence and objective results. On the other hand, it was equally crucial for all to avoid mutual blaming and shaming. No one wanted to be put on the spot, and no one wanted to be summoned to the UN to answer awkward and painful questions. Also, smaller member states were afraid of being overburdened with a complex review process they wouldn't be able to manage. But without a serious and trusted implementation and follow-up process, the whole agenda would easily end up as a meaningless paper tiger. If the SDGs were supposed to ignite a fundamental transformation, then everyone had to be ready to walk the talk. And everyone had to stand ready for being held accountable and for potentially receiving criticism for lack of progress.

Interestingly, the developed countries found themselves in an uncomfortable new situation. Their role in this new agenda was not only to provide funding, as they were used to during the MDG era, but also to come to the UN, like the developing countries and report about their progress or setbacks regarding sustainability. The prospect of being grilled about their own unsustainable production and consumption patterns, about trade restrictions or their domination of international financial institutions led to a considerable paddling back on accountability.[12] Hence, the two co-chairs eventually forged the compromise to establish a review process in the framework of the HLPF where, in addition to regular UN reporting, member states would present their own reviews on a voluntary basis. These Voluntary National Reviews (VNRs), as they would be called, should be followed by a round of questioning by a group of other peer member states. Anything explicitly binding or a mandatory accountability mechanism caused too much unease with both developed and developing countries (Donoghue 2020).

Despite the voluntary character, the new review procedures were quite robust compared to the historically rather weak follow-up on other UN development agreements. Member states had agreed to expose themselves to at least some group and peer pressure and were ready to eventually face some critical questioning in the group discussions. Of course, this was not supposed to be an in-depth independent review, squarely pointing to shortcomings and gaps, let alone issuing binding recommendations. But still, compared to other UN processes, there was hope that it would be a lot more constructive than just a meaningless talk shop. After all, blaming and shaming at the UN in most cases is anyway unlikely to effectively propel more progress and better results in sustainable development.

When the negotiation process was nearing its deadline of Friday, 31 July, the pressure was growing and lobbying was intense. Arguments were thrown back and forth, revised and then again fed into the process, while participants were increasingly struggling with fatigue, wariness, and nervousness. It was clear to all that compromises had to be forged with "pain on all sides" and solutions had to involve "verbal ingenuity and a degree of constructive ambiguity" (Dodds et al. 2017: 97). Especially the last days were intense and tedious. But which ones were the stumbling blocks that kept entrenched delegations fighting over words and phrases? All member states bring their specific concerns and topics to UN negotiations that they eventually want to see reflected in the text. Consequently, this leads to long entreaties and wish lists that at some point inevitably are clashing with those from other delegations. Accommodating all of them comes close to squaring the circle, in particular if one side insists on mentioning a topic, such as sexual and reproductive health and rights, the role of the family or gay, lesbian, and transgender people, and another insists on deleting it. In such difficult cases, the solution usually is to use already agreed language from previous treaties or agreements, or refer to existing charters or conference outcomes. This is, of course, just old wine in new bottles, and in the end basically underscores how entrenched positions are over some topics.

Another thorny issue was the principle of "Common But Differentiated Responsibility" (CBDR). This principle was born in 2012 at the UNFCCC and conceded developing countries less responsibilities in combating climate change as they had contributed a lot less to emissions and pollution. The principle has been acknowledged in nearly all international environmental agreements since then, emphasizing the historical responsibilities of developed countries due to their greater part in global environmental degradation. But now, the G77 and China were insisting on making CBDR a general principle, applicable to the whole new agenda and, thus, to development in general (Donoghue 2020). For some developing countries, CBDR was reflecting the historic injustices and imbalances from which they were still suffering. For others, it was basically a bargaining chip that could be used at will to trade in other concessions in the final outcome package. However, CBDR has more of a symbolic role and in fact doesn't emanate in measurable impact, neither in terms of funding nor in terms of other commitments. No country makes a contribution or commitment or refuses to do so because of CBDR. In addition, this strict separation between developed countries being the perpetrators and developing countries being the victims has long been overtaken and outlived by reality. With some of the middle-income countries having turned into big polluters and environmental sinners themselves, it was increasingly difficult to solely see them in the victim's role, dependent on support from rich countries. Eventually, the compromise was to only reconfirm CBDR in the declaration but without any more details about its specific application. Like CBDR, there were more issues and debates that are hard to fathom, let alone fully understand from an outsider's perspective. UN discussions and documents are filled with wordings in UN speak that only insiders can completely decipher and get the full meaning behind a specific phrase or word. In the end, reaching an agreement boils down to finding "ways in which each group could feel that it had gained and lost in equal measure" (Dodds et al. 2017: 107).

Finally, there was a telling last-minute debate about which group was the most disadvantaged. The SIDS wanted a particular reference to their group under climate finance, which the LDCs bitterly opposed. Once again, it was the fear over losing attention and funding that was driving these confrontations (Dodds et al. 2017: 106–109). Eventually, to accommodate all demands, all developing countries were mentioned in some group or another that deserved particular attention.

In the late afternoon of Sunday, August 2, the last session eventually happily ended with all UN member states agreeing on the document "Transforming Our World: The 2030 Agenda for Sustainable Development." The official adoption followed on September 25, 2015 in the UN General Assembly where the 193 member states of the United Nations adopted the 2030 Agenda for Sustainable Development in consensus.

Those that had been part of the negotiation process were filled with excitement about this far-reaching outcome that three years ago, no one would have ever dreamed of. Many times, the SDGs had been rather running the risk of getting lost in the maize of UN corridors and meeting rooms. When the 2030 Agenda was adopted, delegations were filled with relief, joy, and confidence about having accomplished a major feat. Never before had one agreement so compellingly spelled out the global challenges affecting all countries and being decisive for the future of all, no matter if rich or poor. And never before had all UN member states committed themselves to jointly tackling these challenges with a universal plan that required strong buy-in and engagement by all.

Much appraisal and credit were given to the co-chairs, both of the OWG and the intergovernmental negotiations, and their skillful and careful shepherding of these two processes that led to a win-win outcome rather than a zero-sum game. They crafted attractive and convincing proposals and compromises, and managed to persuade skeptics to eventually accept them (Chasek et al. 2016).

UN member states and the UN community were extremely positive and enthusiastic about this new agenda, like were most of those who had followed the process. Most criticism centered around the 2030 Agenda being too broad and too long, making it hard to fathom its content and even harder to manage. Some pointed out that the SDGs with their 17 goals and 169 targets "represent a return to the "Christmas tree approach" to setting international agendas, which incorporates everything but the kitchen sink, thereby losing any focus and sense of direction" (Fukuda-Parr 2017: 227). With a view to scarce resources and packed political agendas, governments could see themselves forced to prioritize the politically convenient and popular goals and targets, that is the low-hanging fruit of what was achievable and presentable. Or, from a public-relations point of view, governments could be tempted to focus on saving the cutest animals, preparing for the scariest disaster scenarios or responding to the most touching pictures and stories about suffering, whatever was manageable.

This post-2015 journey has been remarkable in many ways: it had produced the first truly global consultations at unprecedented scale. It had gone through a time of deep learning and deep diving into the interlinkages and interdependencies of development and the environment. And it had successfully created an unparalleled degree of transparency, inclusiveness, and openness, in particular with a view to civil society, academia, and the private sector. Altogether, this rather experimental and off-the-script post-2015 process benefited not only the 2030 Agenda and its legitimacy, but also the UN and its processes as a whole. After several UN negotiations in the past years not being able to rise up to the challenges and to produce meaningful results with subsequent action, the 2030 Agenda had delivered so much more than anyone expected in the beginning. The post-2015 process had united the UN and its member states in a unique way, apparently leaving behind historical, ideological divides and initiating a new time where the world would live up to the pressing global challenges. In particular, the OWG and its unusual deep learning exercise had managed to take a lot of heat out of traditional confrontations. Interestingly, with Colombia and others, countries from the Global South had contrived the idea of merging the poverty and the environmental agenda and passionately fought for the SDGs. It was not a solely donors' driven undertaking anymore and, thus, perfectly reflecting how much the global development landscape had changed. It had an unexpected melt-down effect on the usual dividing lines between rich and poor, developed and developing countries. This time of learning for all, dealing with the global nature of poverty, growth, consumption and production, and protecting the environment, paved the way for a new understanding of the necessary fundamental change in human life on earth that had to happen in rich and poor countries all over the world.

In hindsight, those three years and three months between the Rio+20 Conference 2012, starting the post-2015 process, and the UN Development Summit 2015, ending it, were a game-changer for both the development and environmental communities. It was a discovery journey about the nature of the beast of sustainable development and its full impact on societies, economies, and countries. At first, this endeavor looked like a rather uneasy expedition into uncharted territory, swirling through the UN meeting rooms with many participants being rather reluctant and wary about the usefulness and added-value of such an undertaking. But then, this process yielded unexpected power over breaking up entrenched mindsets and long-term held convictions and tenets. It fundamentally put into question the alleged role model of rich countries and their way of life, the benefits-only belief in quick economic development, and turned upside down the relationship between developed and developing countries, as well as the relationship between fighting poverty and protecting the environment. It was straightforwardly laying bare the compelling interlinkages and interdependencies between all societies and economies which made it impossible to not participate or to be ignorant about the challenges.

In the end, the post-2015 process had also made fighting poverty and protecting the environment messier and more complex. It had added a lot of uncertainty, meandered into many forks and had become a cobweb of countless scientific findings, knowledge gaps, and yet to materialize innovations and solutions. Many were left with the feeling that it appeared almost impossible to just set the course for going sustainable and then safely navigate to the land of sustainability. Obviously, there was still so much to learn. It was evident what went wrong and what didn't work. But it was much more difficult to precisely say which one would be the best sustainable solution to a specific challenge as this was very much depending on the advances by science and technology. Affordability, accessibility, and availability at scale also played a role in identifying truly sustainable solutions, and it might take unforeseeable twists and turns and surprises to get there. But despite all uncertainties, the post-2015 process had built up an overarching and widely shared understanding of the mounting sustainability challenges urgently demanding answers and solutions without which every country and society would be facing a daunting future.

Hence, one of the most important conclusions of this whole post-2015 process was that the sustainability journey had actually only just begun. The world was at the very beginning of understanding and working toward a sustainable world with the bulk of research and innovations still ahead. With the 2030 Agenda the world had officially kickstarted that journey and now needed to get down to business.

Financing the SDGs: Who is going to pay for this?

That was the trillion-dollar question during the post-2015 process. All the best intentions and ambitious plans are very likely to end up as meaningless papers unless they are underpinned with specific ways and means, in particular financial means, for implementing them. Thus, at the time when the MDGs were set up, a Financing for Development (FfD) track was initiated to deal with exactly these financing questions. The first Financing for Development Conference was convened in 2002 in Monterrey, Mexico, mostly to serve the implementation of the MDGs. The outcome was the "Monterrey Consensus," an understanding between developed and developing countries about the role of FfD, including private sector investment, economic growth, and market economies, topics which were all still rather unspecific at the time.

But the real revolution in Monterrey was that for the first time finance ministers entered the development world. The second FfD conference took place in Doha, Qatar (2008). Subsequently, when the Rio+20 summit decided to start the post-2015 process, this also required a new financing agreement, building on Monterrey and Doha, to undergird the implementation of the goals and targets. And as there would be many new ambitious goals, it wasn't hard to guess that the price tag would be reaching dwindling highs. But given the very new character of many goals with numerous issues that still had to be explored, it obviously would be extremely difficult to exactly determine the amount and the type of funding needed.

In the MDG era, the development world was structured in a rather clear way: rich countries were supporting the poor ones in their development efforts through bilateral and multilateral assistance. Official Development Assistance (ODA), granted by OECD developed countries since 1970, was supposed to reach 0.7 percent of donors' gross national product (GNP). Only very few countries would match this goal many years later. It was basically a government-to-government partnership. But with time, a certain donor fatigue was setting in, very much driven by economic downturns in industrialized countries and a growing weariness in fighting poverty as, despite all aid, so many people were still mired in misery. Furthermore, many tenets shaping development financing were considerably changing. The once sharp dividing line between donors and recipients was getting increasingly blurred. Long-time recipients were becoming donors themselves, emerging economies were overtaking the per capita GDP of many Western countries, and financial flows from capital markets to the Global South were dwarfing traditional aid assistance. Hence, the post-2015 agenda would be for a very different world compared to the MDG era.

The 2030 Agenda was supposed to be applied to the whole world, propelling change for sustainability in all countries, not only in developing countries. Thus, a traditional donor–recipient agreement, simply leveraging more ODA from donors was obviously outdated and would clearly fall short of what was needed for such a comprehensive agenda. Debating the financing of the SDGs was essentially boiling down to three key questions: how to significantly increase levels of funding, in view of the many new ambitious commitments, how to broaden the variety of resources and forms of funding, given the comprehensive character of this new agenda and the explicit inclusion of economic development, and how to ensure that the money spent would yield the desired transformative results.

To get some high-quality input into the discussion, member states at the Rio+20 summit had decided to set up a specialized group, the Intergovernmental Committee of Experts on Sustainable Development Finance (ICESDF). It comprised 30 experts that should assess financing needs, existing instruments and frameworks, and eventually produce a report with options for financing and implementing the new agenda. The OWG had already taken up this topic but the debates remained rather general and didn't get near any specific conclusion what financing the SDGs could possibly look like. The only consensus from the beginning was that any new FfD agreement had to go decisively beyond simply raising the amount of money; it had to include numerous additional aspects of an enabling environment, such as trade, technology, capacity-building, tackling illicit financial flows, or corruption. While formally the post-2015 negotiations and the FfD negotiations were two separate tracks, they both were intertwined by nature as obviously neither would be able to produce a meaningful result without the other.

The months before and during the FfD negotiations witnessed numerous discussions trying to assess how much money would be needed for the SDGs. At the IMF–World Annual Meetings in 2014, at a session about "Financing Development Post-2015", organized by multilateral development banks, experts presented their estimates that the SDGs would cost three times as much as the MDGs. If the world was serious about the SDGs, so the conclusion at the IMF meeting, either a doubling of developing countries' tax revenues was needed or a doubling of aid flows. They called on the world to face the need to go big in financing, otherwise the 2030 Agenda would remain a promise on paper, without any chance of triggering the envisaged impact and transformation. The Sustainable Development Solutions Network (SDSN), an experts' network, had estimated that it would cost $2–3 trillion a year to achieve the SDGs with $1.5 trillion spending in low and middle-income countries alone. Other UN sources outlined that the cost of achieving the SDGs would be about $3.3–4.5 trillion a year. The United Nations Conference on Trade and Development (UNCTAD) estimated that annual investment requirements in infrastructure alone (water, telecommunications, energy, transport, buildings, etc.) in all countries amounted between $5 and 7 trillion. Almost $4 trillion would be needed in developing countries, of which roughly only one-fourth was available (Martin 2015; SDG Fund 2015: 7; UNCTAD 2014).

One crucial input, sketching out the brave new development financing world, came from the World Bank and the IMF. The title "From Billions to Trillions" already summarized what needed to happen. It also highlighted the new reality of the economic landscape with the six largest middle-income countries (MICs) accounting roughly the same share of global GDP as the six largest high-income countries. It equally stressed the growing role and potential of private finance. While ODA would remain the main source of financing for the LDCs, so the report, MICs could unlock much more funding through tapping into private financial flows and, in particular, providing a conducive investment environment (World Bank/IMF 2015: 1–10).

The sheer numbers were simply mindblowing, and it appeared highly unlikely that countries in need, in particular the poorest, would really be showered with that much money. Also, it was difficult to understand how these spiraling calculations could be broken down to specific critical investments. Developed countries, naturally, argued that middle-income countries should take over more responsibility in supporting the poor countries given their development progress over the past years. The G77 and China clearly rejected this argument, firmly defending their recipient status even though the realities in particular in the emerging economies had considerably changed. Their strong urge of not being punished for development progress had merit but, in fact, followed a popular and well-known political negotiating tactic of never ever voluntarily giving up financial support. However, in view of the global character of the new agenda that was demanding change from every country and the fundamentally altered donor–recipient relationship, it was obvious that traditional aid from OECD donors or public funding alone would never ignite the envisaged transformation.

Also, experience had widely shown that just chipping in more funding didn't come with the guarantee that more money would do more good, or that more funding would necessarily have the desired additional impact. Thus, improving effectiveness and results-orientation, and identifying innovative and smart financing solutions was the real challenge that concurrently had to be tackled by raising the levels of funding. One of the major lessons learned from the MDGs, but also from the Rio agreements, was that a supporting policy framework and institutional capacities had long been underestimated as being decisive for making effective use of financial resources. Hence, an adequate institutional environment and good governance were prerequisites for enhancing effective financing (World Bank Group 2013: 4–6; World Bank/IMF 2015: 21–22).

When deciding about the date for the final conference for the new FfD agreement, it came as a surprise to many, that the developing countries had managed to push the UN General Assembly to set the date for July 2015, while the 2030 Agenda should be adopted at the UN General Assembly in September 2015: the final conference for adopting the agreement about how and how much to finance was scheduled two months prior to the agreement about what to finance. One would have expected it the other way round, but many developing countries were driven by a deep-rooted fear that otherwise the financing negotiations would not get the necessary public attention and pressure, once the 2030 Agenda was concluded. In hindsight, they were probably right. After the excitement of having adopted the 2030 Agenda, it most probably would have been extremely difficult to get back to negotiating seemingly secondary issues such as financing or other technical support.

The final new FfD agreement was set to be adopted in Addis Ababa, Ethiopia, thus, the new financing agreement would be called the Addis Ababa Action Agenda. The experts' group scheduled three drafting sessions between January and July 2015. One of the key issues during these sessions was the not unfounded fear of developing countries that development finance would lose out against environment and climate finance, thus, hollowing out the fight against poverty. Subsequently, developing countries even proposed to introduce a separate accounting for development finance and climate finance, respectively. Developing countries were keen on not accepting anything that could let the developed countries off the hook and lessen their responsibility for providing public funding for development. The G77 repeatedly stressed the importance of CBDR and demanded from the developed countries to comply with their responsibilities. Private sector engagement or enhanced domestic efforts to increase revenues were most welcome on top, but this should under no circumstances be used as an excuse to reduce ODA (Dodds et al. 2017: 117–120).

Like during the negotiations on the SDGs, there was the same competition about which group was the neediest. The LDCs, SIDS, MICs, and the African countries all made their claims with the two latter groups making the point that they were home to the highest numbers of poor people. In particular, the MICs were afraid of losing their status as a recipient and, thus, being cut off from donor aid. Eventually to accommodate all, like in the final 2030 Agenda text, all developing countries were mentioned as belonging to some group that deserved particular attention.

As a lot of money was at stake for many countries and many economies, several issues remained open and contentious and had to be resolved during the final days on the spot in the Ethiopian capital. The drama of the expected showdown in Addis in July 2015 was underscored by the number of participants alone. Over 11,000 people headed to the conference, including 18 heads of state and government and many more ministers. After three intense days, where tensions were running high with the negotiations at the brink of failure, eventually, a deal on the new financing agreement was struck.

Overall, the Addis Agenda contained seven action areas of which the first three were the most important: domestic public resources, mobilizing the private sector, and development cooperation.

The chapter on domestic public resources, about how to enable the developing countries to boost the flow of tax revenues and other income was surprisingly self-critical. In fact, official language about financing had never been so outspoken before that developing countries could do a lot more themselves to generate more revenues. This would significantly reduce their aid dependency and create more fiscal space for themselves to set their own priorities and implement policies (Martin 2015). Comparing the median tax revenue showed a huge gap between developed and developing countries. While since 2000, the richest countries had an average tax revenue of 22–25 percent of GDP, the poorest have been hovering between 10 and 14 percent. They weren't even close to what would be considered a solid level of revenues for treasuries (United Nations, Inter-agency Task Force on Financing for Development 2020: 37–40). In fact, more than one-third of all developing countries and more than 60 percent of countries affected by fragility, conflict, and violence were far below that threshold. Hence, increasing the tax-to-GDP ratio through, for example, broadening and deepening the tax base or improving systems of taxation, closing loopholes, and significantly strengthening tax administrations was dearly needed (World Bank Group 2013: 9–10, 2018: 27).

Regarding the framing conditions for financing, Addis was quite outspoken and very clear about the need for an enabling environment, that is adequate public policies, a stable and transparent regulatory framework, and accountable institutions as well as sound macroeconomic and financial policies promoting sustainable development. It was, in fact, a call for providing incentives for attracting and channeling sustainable investments, changing consumption and production patterns and for harnessing the potential of science, technology, and innovation for the SDGs. This was effectively homework the delegations were giving to themselves as in the end this was for each country to decide about their own domestic economic, fiscal and financial policies and regulations.

The chapter about mobilizing the private sector described one of the most complex but also controversial challenges with many unbeaten paths still to explore. For a long time, the private sector had been broadly associated with profit and rent-seeking to the detriment of poor people and development objectives (IISD – Earth Negotiations Bulletin 1997). But over time, the relationship between the United Nations, government-led processes and the private sector has considerably changed, giving way to a much better mutual understanding about the common interests and the potential for synergies and a mutually beneficial relationship. The creation of the UN Global Compact[13] in 2000 and the unanimous endorsement of the UN Guiding Principles on Business and Human Rights[14] in 2011 were some milestones, reshaping the cooperation between the UN system and the corporate world. But these were just sketching out some principles and tenets, outlining what responsible commitment by the private sector should look like. They were far from incentivizing any targeted investments or any specific other mandatory commitments to be reached.

In the meantime, a new reality on the ground had materialized shaped by foreign direct investments, flows from private funds, foundations, and remittances. Especially in middle-income countries, foreign direct investment flows have grown many times larger than aid, and remittances alone were roughly more than three times the amount of ODA. They play an often overlooked but considerable role, and since many years dwarf traditional aid. In 2015, ODA comprised roughly 15 percent of all external financing. Breaking this down to the different groups of developing countries, revealed a little surprising picture: in LDCs, ODA accounted for almost two-thirds of their external financing, in lower middle-income countries less than 20 percent and in upper middle-income countries less than 5 percent. The more a country managed to reduce poverty and develop its economy, the more that country was able to attract financial flows from the private sector and access international capital markets (Chhibber 2016: 9; World Bank Group 2013: 23–24). Within a decade, roughly 30 countries had moved up from low- to middle-income status, and a growing number of those once poor and now middle-income countries had even become donors, lenders and investors themselves.

The agreed text about the private sector in the Addis Agenda, in the end, came close to an almost visionary dream about the public and private sector working hand in hand for the same good. It was picturing an ideal about harnessing the development potential of a dynamic and well-functioning business sector for employment and a thriving economy. But Addis didn't really go much beyond that, falling short of specific proposals how to involve a rent-seeking, profit-oriented private sector that didn't necessarily subscribe to all sustainable development principles and objectives (Caliari 2015). In fact, the wording of Addis to "call on all businesses to apply their creativity and innovation to solving sustainable development challenges ... [and to] ... invite them to engage as partners in the development process" were the right cues but disappointingly didn't usher in more specific actionable goals. The Addis text talked a lot about encouraging, promoting or exploring but left it with that (United Nations 2015).

Another key topic in Addis was the far too little action on combating illicit financial flows, corruption, tax evasion, and fraud as well as on implementing an effective fiscal system. Addis underscored that serious engagement regarding these shortcomings was overdue. If addressed appropriately, the estimated impact could be huge: the OECD had quantified that tax avoidance resulted in revenue losses of between $100 billion and $240 billion annually. UNCTAD reported that developing countries alone lost $100 billion a year as a result of profit shifting, amounting to one-third of their corporate tax base (Ocampo 2016: 2).

The topic taxes also ushered in a last-minute controversial discussion with the developing countries calling for a new global tax body. The idea was to tackle tax evasion, in particular by multinational corporations that dodge paying taxes in the countries they operate, through a new international tax body. There was some momentum for this idea. But major differences about which would be the appropriate host institution and most developed countries being extremely wary of a regulatory overshoot and a possible UN tax authority prevented an agreement (Anderson/Chonghaile 2015).

The development cooperation chapter was certainly an integral crucial part of the new financing agreement that Addis couldn't have done without. But it was also by far the least newsworthy and innovative. It basically reconfirmed the 0.7 ODA commitment from 1970, repeatedly re-endorsed throughout the years but never achieved. In 2023, globally ODA had reached 0.37 percent, staying far below the 0.7 pledge. Developing countries were particularly disappointed, as no new money was put on the table, only a 45-year-old 0.7 ODA promise simply reiterated, and again without any timeline.

The most surprising and very specific decision was to incorporate a climate-financing provision, agreed in the context of the UNFCCC, that was also repeated in target 13.a of the 2030 Agenda. The not unfounded fear of developing countries that ODA would eventually lose out against climate finance was eventually met with an additional $100 billion per year pledge for climate adaptation that developed countries should provide for developing countries by 2020. This additional funding, which was one of the few measurable commitments in the Addis Agenda, would be over and above existing ODA for developing countries. In the follow-up, this climate spending target proved to be extremely valuable for holding donors accountable.

The final chapter about data, measuring and monitoring was very much building on the lessons learned from the MDG era where sound measuring, based on reliable and comparable data, was still fairly underdeveloped. Thus, specifically dedicating resources to statistical offices to improve the measuring of development progress, was one of the most overlooked but important steps decided in Addis. The role and impact of data and measuring will be discussed in more detail in the next chapter.

After signing the Addis Agenda in July 2015, the diplomatic crowd returned to New York to finalize the negotiations on the SDGs. Interestingly, back in New York a rather tedious discussion ensued about the relationship between the Addis Agreement and the 2030 Agenda and its chapter about the means of implementation. Eventually, the Addis Agenda was explicitly referenced in the 2030 Agenda and some of the Addis language incorporated. However, most developing countries were not happy with the Addis outcome as in their view the rich countries had not only failed to live up to their obligation to meet their old ODA commitments but also to further upscale them given the ambition of the 2030 Agenda. Historically, the UN system and the poverty agenda had been built on ODA as the very basic financing mechanism. Nurtured and cultivated over many years, a deep-rooted thinking had been prevailing that public money provided by traditional donors was the key factor deciding about growth and development. But now "delegates had to move beyond a seventy-year-old negotiating pattern around ODA" (Kamau et al. 2018: 235). Hence, exploring financing beyond ODA meant for the UN, and also governments, treading the unbeaten path of international capital markets where they would be facing tough competition and return-on-investment calculations.

In hindsight, the Addis Agenda certainly wasn't the big leap forward in reaching the next level of development financing. And in the following years, it became obvious that Addis was summarily inadequate for mobilizing the additional resources needed. But despite all shortcomings, the Addis Agenda was an ideological watershed moment in financing, "a turning point for ODA ... [and] an increased role for the private sector in development finance" (Dodds et al. 2017: 120). Both the development and the environmental community had never been so ready before to see the private sector as a partner. The Doha FfD agreement in 2008 had already cautiously acknowledged that the role of ODA in catering to financing needs would be decreasing, while the private sector would gain more importance. But with the ambitious 2030 Agenda, there was no doubt left that partnering up with the private sector was indispensable as otherwise the trillions needed to achieve the SDGs would never be mobilized. The Addis Agenda had significantly broadened the plethora of options beyond public financing and ways of leveraging money and impact, not properly thought of before. And the aftermath of Addis would subsequently trigger a sheer explosion of initiatives regarding private sector engagement that will be analyzed in more detail in the next chapter.

What was conspicuously missing in the Addis agreement, however, were specific spending and other quantified targets regarding specific quantified results. It would have been extremely desirable, for example, to have specific quantified targets for domestic resource mobilization, relevant in many poor countries, such as reaching a sound tax-to-GDP ratio, expanding the tax base, or reducing corporate tax avoidance. The same applied to financial inclusion that was given prominence in the Addis Agenda but failed to provide specific and measurable targets, for example, about the percentage of women, minorities, or vulnerable people that should have access to financial services (Chhibber 2016: 3–11). Disappointingly, many crucial points that were good in substance weren't broken down to figures and numbers what the envisaged change should look like. Undergirding the single SDGs with spending targets, for example, would have made the subsequent tracing and tracking of progress in implementing the single SDGs much more substantial. Also, the specific linkages between the SDGs and the Addis Agenda were not really clear, and partially completely missing. There was no general logic or structure how the specific Addis provisions should support the single SDGs (Elder et al. 2016).

Despite the Addis Agenda laying the ground for a major expansion of the development equation, it disappointingly didn't go much beyond recognizing that differentiated forms of financing and other enabling means needed to be explored and fleshed out. Also, while everyone was clear about the necessity to enhance the quality, impact, and effectiveness of provided resources, Addis didn't manage to produce new or groundbreaking proposals on how to achieve this. The final text was basically rife with what would be promising, thinkable and desirable, but then leaving it to others to take it from there and explore the concrete options. More was politically not possible. The high pressure to reach an agreement before the adoption of the 2030 Agenda that was still being negotiated in parallel and hadn't been finalized yet might have played a role in leaving the Addis Agenda rather weak and generic. But it was also the minimum that the delegations had to produce for a meaningful outcome. Had Addis produced less, this probably would have cast an enormous shadow on the SDGs to be adopted only a few weeks later.

Notes

1 https://www.beyond2015.org/world-we-want-2015-web-platform/
2 https://about.myworld2030.org/my-world-2015/

3 https://www.undp.org/publications/global-conversation-begins-emerging-views-new-development-agenda
4 https://unsdg.un.org/resources/million-voices-world-we-want
5 https://www.un-ilibrary.org/content/books/9789210562119
6 Statement by Ambassador Masood Khan, https://sustainabledevelopment.un.org/content/documents/6315pakistan1.pdf
7 Statement by Ambassador Anna Brandt, https://sustainabledevelopment.un.org/content/documents/6535sweden2.pdf
8 Statement by Ambassador Sofia Borges, https://sustainabledevelopment.un.org/content/documents/6540timor.pdf
9 Statement by Ambassador Manjeev Singh Puri, https://sustainabledevelopment.un.org/content/documents/3428india.pdf
10 Statement on behalf of the African Group, March 14, 2013, https://sustainabledevelopment.un.org/content/documents/3423africangroup.pdf
11 China provides consistent political support to the G77 but doesn't consider itself a member.
12 For example the statement by Spain: Intervención a Cargo del Secretario General de Cooperación Internacional para el Desarrollo Don Gonzalo Robles Orozco, https://sustainabledevelopment.un.org/content/documents/3434spain.pdf
13 https://unglobalcompact.org/
14 https://www.business-humanrights.org/en/big-issues/un-guiding-principles-on-business-human-rights/

References

Anderson, Mark/Clár Ní Chonghaile (2015): Addis Ababa Development Finance Summit: All You Need to Know. The Guardian, July 16, 2015.

Caballero, Paula/Patti Londoño (2022): *Redefining Development. The Extraordinary Genesis of the Sustainable Development Goals*, Boulder/London: Lynne Rienner Publishers.

Caliari, Aldo (2015): Investing in the SDGs: Whose Business? In: United Nations Research Institute for Social Development: The Road to Addis and Beyond, https://www.unrisd.org/road-to-addis-caliari

Chasek, Pamela/Lynn M. Wagner/Faye Leone/Ana-Maria Lebada/Nathalie Risse (2016): Getting to 2030: Negotiating the Post-2015 Sustainable Development Agenda, Wiley Online Library, April 25, 2016. https://doi.org/10.1111/reel.12149

Chhibber, Ajay (2016): *Assessing and Evaluating the Addis Ababa Action Agenda*, New Delhi: National Institute of Public Finance and Policy.

Dodds, Felix/David Donoghue/Jimena Leiva Roesch (2017): *Negotiating the Sustainable Development Goals, a* Transformational *Agenda for an Insecure World*, Oxon/New York: Routledge.

Donoghue, David (2020): Die Verhandlungen zur Agenda 2030 für nachhaltige Entwicklung, in: Vereinte Nationen, 5/2020. The Negotiations on the Agenda 2030 for Sustainable Development. Vereinte Nationen.

Elder, Mark/Magnus Bengtsson/Lewis Akenji (2016): An Optimistic Analysis of the Means of Implementation for Sustainable Development Goals: Thinking About Goals as Means. *Institute for Global Environmental Strategies, Sustainability*, Vol. 8, No. 9, p. 962. https://doi.org/10.3390/su8090962

Fukuda-Parr, Sakiko (2017): *Millennium Development Goals. Ideas, Interests and Influence*, London/ New York: Routledge.

IISD – Earth Negotiations Bulletin (1997): *Summary Report*, 23-27 June 1997.

Kamau, Macharia/Pamela Chasek/David O'Connor (2018): *Transforming Multilateral Diplomacy. The Inside* Story *of the Sustainable Development Goals*, Oxon/New York: Routledge.

Kjørven, Olav (2016): The Unlikely Journey to the 2030 Agenda for Sustainable Development, IMPAKTER Essay, December 8, 2016. https://impakter.com/impakter-essay-unlikely-journey-2030-agenda-sustainable-development/

Ladd, Paul (2016): Outcome Evaluation of the UNDP Project "Building the Post-2015 Development Agenda: Open and Inclusive Consultations", MDF Training & Consultancy BV, April 2016.

Martin, Matthew (2015): Beyond Addis: How Can We Finance the SDGs? 8 September 2015, in: United Nations Research Institute for Social Development: The Road to Addis and Beyond. https://www.unrisd.org/road-to-addis-martin

Ocampo, José Antonio (2016): The Contribution of the Addis Ababa Action Agenda to the Agenda 2030, Friedrich-Ebert-Stiftung, Perspective, FES New York, March 2016.

SDG Fund (2015): *Business and the United Nations, Working Together Towards the Sustainable Development Goals: A Framework for Action*, Cambridge, MA: Harvard Kennedy School CSR Initiative and Inspiris Limited.

UNCTAD (2014): World Investment Report, United Nations, Geneva. https://unctad.org/en/pages/PressRelease.aspx?OriginalVersionID=194

UNDESA (2014): TST Issues Briefs, a Compendium of Issues Briefs Prepared by the United Nations Inter-Agency Technical Support Team for the United Nations General Assembly Open Working Group on Sustainable Development Goals, New York.

United Nations (2014): The road to dignity by 2030: ending poverty, transforming all lives and protecting the planet. Synthesis report of the Secretary-General on the post-2015 sustainable development agenda, A/69/700, 4 December 2014.

United Nations (2015): Addis Ababa Action Agenda of the Third International Conference on Financing for Development, Addis Ababa, Ethiopia, 13–16 July 2015.

United Nations, Inter-agency Task Force on Financing for Development (2020): Financing for Sustainable Development Report 2020, New York.

United Nations/World Bank (2018): *Pathways for Peace: Inclusive Approaches to Preventing Violent Conflict*, Washington D.C: World Bank.

World Bank Group (2013): *Financing for Development Post-2015*, Washington D.C.: World Bank, October 2013.

World Bank Group (2018): *Implementing the 2030 Agenda*, Washington D.C.: World Bank.

World Bank/International Monetary Fund (IMF) (2015): *From Billions to Trillions: Transforming Development Finance*, Washington DC, April 2, 2015.

4

IMPLEMENTING THE SDGs

Going sustainable and putting into practice 17 goals and 169 targets

The devil lies in the detail of SDG data: You have to measure what you treasure

An adage says that you have to measure what you treasure or only what gets measured, gets done. Recurring to quantifiable and measurable data is much more than a trend; it is increasingly the currency to inform real-world policy decisions. Using quality data and sound measuring means to get an evidence-based picture of the reality on the ground, who is in need, what is missing, what exactly is the human impact on nature, and what kind of action is needed to effectively remedy the situation. It is also essential for evaluating, if the desired results are being produced. In light of limited funding, it is even more important to know how to effectively use resources, monitor progress or setbacks, assess the impact of policies and programs, and ensure accountability for results. Likewise, data and measuring add decisively to the scientific evidence about the functioning of natural ecosystems and the impact of human life on earth. In fact, quantifying and measuring contributes significantly to having an objective picture of the state of play of the social, economic, and environmental reality, and about sustainable development in general.

During the Millennium Development Goals (MDGs) era, the lack of data and the lack of soundly measured results had always been a major shortcoming. The regular MDG reports were, in fact, mostly projections and estimates with poor-quality, scientifically often flawed data. Crucial gaps in measuring and blank spaces in policy planning had been filled only quite late in the 15-year implementation period. Some numbers illustrate the deficient data situation at the time: Between 2002 and 2011, in Sub-Sahara Africa 61 percent of the countries were lacking adequate data to monitor poverty. A UN analysis of 22 MDG indicators revealed that the number of countries reporting on two or more data

DOI: 10.4324/9781032702681-4

points for at least 16 indicators rose rather slowly from 4 countries in 2003 to 129 countries in 2013. Only about two-thirds of the developing countries had half or less of the data available to track and analyze spending on the MDGs. Throughout most of the MDG era, it remained a challenge to trace the funding in different sectors, in particular who was benefiting from the money spent (Martin/Walker 2015: 52–57; United Nations 2015: 10–12).

During the post-2015 negotiations, right from the start the availability or rather dearth of data was a crucial topic. There was broad consensus about the need for better data on health, education, or the economy. However, issues such as human rights, governance, or inclusive societies, appearing as rather political and not measurable, triggered considerable controversy, how they should be incorporated, if at all. The delegations being critical, often argued with their political nature and, thus, the impossibility to draft meaningful goals and targets about human rights or governance. But others, in particular the UN agencies and the Western countries, passionately argued this was the opportunity to develop new objective measures for social realities. Setting new goals on human rights or governance would forcefully stimulate new or improved data and measuring tools for complex social issues (UNDESA 2014: 7). The indicators supposed to underpin the targets to measure their implementation were not negotiated in the post-2015 process and, thus, not under member states' control. Hence, some delegations were afraid to end up with a set of indicators missing the right content, some were afraid to end up with a watered-down and low-ambition set, and others were afraid to end up with a costly and work-intense set of indicators that would overwhelm statistical offices. Usually, defining indicators is a technical work, undertaken by the UN Statistical Commission. But during the post-2015 process, sensitivities were extremely high, and some member states found it hard to see something as purely technical. They were wary of the UN agencies not fully respecting the carefully balanced political compromises of the new goals and targets. Subsequently, in March 2015, a new group was established at the UN, comprising around 30 member states and various UN agencies, called Interagency and Expert Group on Sustainable Development Goal Indicators (IAEG-SDGs). Some delegations were even pushing for treating the indicators as part of the political negotiations. Although not being successful, the agencies, despite having the expertise, eventually found themselves largely relegated to an observer status in the IAEG (Kapto 2019: 135).

Agreeing on the appropriate number of indicators was equally difficult. On the one hand, the SDGs were much more complex and their scope was much wider than the predecessor MDG framework. Thus, a more detailed set of indicators to capture all that the agenda encompassed appeared imperative. On the other hand, there was the danger of overburdening statistical offices with new indicators and new statistical methodologies. Countries could end up being lost in the data jungle and missing out on effectively measuring the SDGs. Debates floated between just having one indicator per target, that is to say less than 200, to keep it manageable, and 500 indicators to ensure proper measuring, as suggested by some experts (MacFeely 2020: 363–365). In the end, the final set comprised 226 indicators. To recall the comparison with the MDGs: These consisted of 8 goals, 21 targets, and 60 indicators; the SDGs consist of 17 goals, 169 targets, and after some amendments 231 indicators.

As the goals and targets covered many fields that had never been measured before and, thus, were not covered by available official statistics and databases, the indicators were grouped into three tiers:

Tier I: the indicator is conceptually clear, has an internationally established methodology, standards are available, and data are regularly produced for at least 50 percent of the countries and of the population in every region where the indicator is relevant (that was applicable to over 40 percent of all indicators);

Tier II: the indicator is conceptually clear, has an internationally established methodology, standards are available but data are not regularly produced by countries (that was applicable to over 20 percent); and

Tier III: no internationally established methodology or standards are yet available for the indicator, but methodology/standards are being (or will be) developed or tested (that was applicable to almost 35 percent).

That basically meant that at the beginning of the SDG era, roughly one-third of the goals and targets were lacking the relevant data and the ways and means to measure them. The IAEG was working intensely on filling these gaps. By 2022, tier I category could be expanded to over 66 percent of all indicators, tier II to over 34 percent, some indicators fell into multiple tier categories, and there were no exclusive tier III indicators left. These were tremendous advances. However, that still meant that for 34 percent of the indicators (tier II) data was available for less than half of the countries worldwide.

Defining indicators is, in fact, a distillation process with the aim of reducing complex reality into simple scores or proxies that should be easy to understand, communicate and, of course, to measure. The specific challenge is to find the right balance between simplicity and complexity. Having an agenda with fewer indicators makes monitoring and measuring easier, faster and more focused. Having more and comprehensive indicators, provides a fuller and more differentiated picture of the reality on the ground but, naturally, requires more work-intensive and complex monitoring and measuring. As many SDGs were hard-fought political compromises, it was critical to translate them into indicators that captured faithfully the essence of the agreed goals and targets. Neither could they reinterpret them, nor could they compensate for weak, watered-down goals and targets.

Unsurprisingly, the political haggling over the SDGs had produced some fuzzy or overloaded targets that were the result of some face-saving compromise or of incorporating and satisfying differing perspectives (van Vuuren et al. 2022). This caused the statisticians some headaches in translating them into meaningful indicators. Some examples illustrate the specific challenges and difficulties:

Clear targets are, for example, target 1.1 ("eradicate extreme poverty ... currently measured as people living on less than $1.25 a day"), target 3.2 ("end preventable deaths of newborns and children under 5 years of age"), or target 6.1 ("achieve universal and equitable access to safe and affordable drinking water for all"). They contain specific quantified results to be reached and reflect crucial parts of social reality, in these cases poverty and wellbeing. Other targets, however, fail to delineate a quantifiable threshold to be crossed. Instead, they rather advocate for new policies or processes or call for continued engagement. Examples for such fuzzy targets are 4.7 ("ensure that all learners acquire the knowledge and skills needed to promote sustainable development"), target 8.3 ("Promote development-oriented policies that support productive activities, decent job creation, entrepreneurship, creativity and innovation"), target 9.5 ("Enhance scientific research, upgrade the technological capabilities of industrial sectors in all countries"), or target 10.2 ("empower and promote the social, economic and political inclusion of all"). These targets define no specific quantifiable results to be reached, thus, it's hard to tell when these would be achieved. Also, they remain rather vague. For example, in target 4.7, it's not clear who the learners are and which knowledge or skills should be acquired; in target 8.3, it's not clear which policies would be covered; or in target 9.5, it's not clear which technological capabilities would be relevant (Svizzero/Tisdell 2015: 22).

Other targets are overloaded with too many objectives to be achieved, for example, target 1.4 ("ensure that all men and women ... have ... access to basic services, ownership and control over land and other forms of property, inheritance, natural resources, appropriate new technology and financial services, including microfinance"). The two eventually selected indicators (indicator 1.4.1: proportion of population living in households with access to basic services; indicator 1.4.2: proportion of total adult population with secure tenure rights to land) cover basic services and land rights. Inheritance, natural resources, new technologies and financial services were simply left out (MacFeely 2020: 363–364).

The measurability of SDG 16 (peaceful societies) had been, from the beginning of the negotiations, a major bone of contention. Eventually, the majority of the SDG 16 targets ended up being quite broad and general, except the very concise target 16.9 ("provide legal identity for all, including birth registration"). The rule of law (target 16.3) is supposed to be measured by the proportion of victims of violence (indicator 16.3.1), unsentenced detainees as a proportion of people in prison (indicator 16.3.2) and proportion of people who accessed a dispute resolution mechanism (indicator 16.3.3). However, other crucial aspects are left out, such as equality of all people before the law, independence of the judiciary, or the quality of independent redress and law enforcement. Effective, accountable, and transparent institutions (target 16.6) are supposed to be measured by government expenditures as a proportion of original approved government budget (indicator 16.6.1) and the proportion of people satisfied with their last experience of public services (indicator 16.6.2). Obviously, these indicators can produce only a very fragmented picture of the functioning of public institutions.

Rather innovative were indicators 16.1.4 ("proportion of population that feel safe walking alone around the area they live after dark") and 16.7.2 ("proportion of population who believe decision-making is inclusive and responsive"). Much of peace or governance is subject to how they are perceived rather than technically measured outputs. For example, if people feel safe says a lot more about the security situation than the number of police or security patrolling the streets. It took some controversial debates until delegations eventually agreed on incorporating these new types of perception indicators.

In the past years there has been an explosion of new approaches to construct indices assessing complex issues, such as governance, democracy, or freedom. The Worldwide Governance Indicators (WGI),[1] the World Press Freedom Index,[2] the Academic Freedom Index,[3] the Corruption Perceptions Index by Transparency International,[4] the Varieties of Democracy Index,[5] or the reports by Freedom House[6] on people's access to political rights and civil liberties are some examples. Each of these, trying to unbundle governance in very different contexts of social reality, has its strengths and weaknesses, and all of them have received both strong appreciation and extensive criticism (Kaufmann 2021).

The MDGs were reporting progress at the country level, thus leaving out developments within countries and societies. However, national statistics often masked geographical areas or groups of societies not benefiting from progress. While national data was telling a success story, data disaggregated by sex, age, income, location, ethnicity, or other relevant characteristics could tell quite a different story. There could be a small elite harvesting the fruits of growth, while considerable scores of the population were left behind, leading to a widening gap between a few rich and many poor. Hence, the need to disaggregate data was one of the lessons learned from the MDGs that was translated into the SDGs (UNDP 2016: 46–51). In order to get a more nuanced picture about poverty, the World Bank in 2017 introduced two complementary global poverty lines with some updates in 2022. In lower-middle-income countries, the poverty line was set at $3.65, and in upper-middle-income countries at $6.85 per person per day. In many MICs, average prosperity levels had risen so much that people were poor and couldn't make ends meet, if they lived on $6.85 a day. The global extreme poverty rate of $1.90 was raised to $2.15 per person per day. Anyone living on $2.15 or less is considered living in extreme poverty.[7]

Another lesson learned from the MDGs, that was taken up by the SDGs, was the need for quality of results. It is comparatively easy to state, if education, health, or jobs are available or missing. But equally important is assessing, if they are accessible to all, affordable, or if they are provided at a quality level. The number of children in school doesn't say anything about what they learn. Or the number of hospitals doesn't say anything about the quality of health services they provide or if people can afford them.

All goals, targets, and indicators were assigned with custodian UN and other international agencies that are responsible for tracking progress and producing regular reports. After a couple of years, the custodians pointedly disclosed more and more gaps in quality, reliability, and comparability of data and measuring. For example, the World Bank and the World Health Organization, the custodians on target 7.1 about access to affordable, reliable and modern energy services, underscored the need for a meaningful definition what access to energy looks like, taking into account that in particular in low-income countries (LICs) and in situations of fragility, conflict, and violence, data are often not available, reliable, and comparable (IEA et al. 2024: 142). The International Renewable Energy Agency (IRENA) and the OECD, custodians on target 7.a about the financial flows to developing countries in support of clean energy, bemoan a lack of centralization of data collection and standardization of commitments which still makes it difficult to track and compare the impact of financial flows (IEA et al. 2024: 146). The United Nations Office on Drugs and Crime (UNODC) and UNCTAD, the custodians on indicator 16.4.1 about measuring illicit financial flows, in 2023 produced the first official estimates of illicit financial flows in nine countries, based on new statistical concepts they had developed. More pilot testing until 2026 is supposed to deliver a more real-time picture of the impact of illicit financial flows (United Nations, Inter-agency Task Force on Financing for Development 2024: 57). And UNODC, responsible for target 16.5 about reducing corruption and bribery, published in 2023 a new framework to measure corruption with an overwhelming number of 145 indicators.[8]

Ensuring sound measuring and comparability of data remains a challenge. More than 70 percent of statistical offices in low- and lower-middle-income countries see themselves ill-equipped to properly measure the SDGs. Registering every birth and death, for example, the most basic statistic, is still not happening in every place, in particular in Sub-Sahara Africa. One billion people worldwide remain without official proof of identity. Countries, such as Syria, Yemen, or North Korea, have no survey data and highly unreliable data. And often the poorest and neediest are elusive to official statistics because they may be homeless, may live in slums or war zones, or may be refugees or belong to socially stigmatized groups (Stuart et al. 2016: 44–45; World Bank Group 2021: 59–60). For the cross-cutting SDGs 5 (gender equality), 13 (climate change), and 16 (peaceful societies and effective institutions), less than half of the 193 countries produce data that are internationally comparable (United Nations 2023a: 8–11). While the goals and targets emanating from the MDGs about poverty, health, or education had the advantage of benefiting from years of experience, in particular the goals covering the quite new economic dimension are comparatively weak and leave out many crucial aspects.

In recent years, measuring and assessing environmental sustainability have undergone an astonishing development with quantum leaps of scientific progress. Before the 2000s, sustainability was more a way of life and a feel-good factor, critical of the popular single-use mentality and fast consumption cycles, but less a quantifiable science. Since then, new metrics, measures, and data have conquered various research fields, and sustainability assessment tools are being designed for almost all aspects of life. They are capturing in real time what is produced, used, emitted, or discarded. The use of new data sources, such as earth observation data or satellite images, will even further enhance evidence-based decision-making, improving the availability, quality and timeliness of data. In fact, it has never been easier to assess if something was sustainable, and it has never been easier to demystify and disclose the full impact of once hailed success stories of industrialization and rampant economic growth.

There are more and more ecolabels and other sustainability initiatives that certify products and services that are sourced, produced, and provided in a sustainable way. Forest Stewardship Council,[9] Marine Stewardship Council,[10] Fair Trade,[11] Leadership in Energy and Environmental Design (LEED),[12] or the Happy Planet Index (HPI)[13] are just a few to mention. And new indexes and ways of measuring environmental sustainability are continuously being worked on. The Environmental Sustainability Index, first published in 2000, and since 2006 called Environmental Performance Index (EPI),[14] published every two years, is providing a ranking of almost all countries regarding their performance on tackling climate change, environmental health, and ecosystem vitality.

In the same vein, there are various approaches redefining measuring economic performance while taking into account sustainability. The measure of Gross Domestic Product (GDP) has lost much of its former role. Although it was always intended as a measure for economic activity only, over the years it morphed into a proxy for wellbeing and progress. GDP growth was supposed to be good for the whole economy and, thus, for everyone. But growth comes with boon and bane, in particular from an environmental point of view. "Beyond GDP" refers to a longstanding debate among mainstream economists aimed at developing indicators of progress that are as clear and compelling as GDP but in addition include other measures of wellbeing, such as environmental, social and quality-of-life aspects.

The data revolution, ubiquitous in all aspects of life, is moving forward and is increasingly shaping and framing the sustainability journey. If the world wants to go sustainable, this means that a myriad of information and data needs to be collected on a regular basis, compiled, aggregated, analyzed and then fed into decision-making processes and policies. And measuring and comparing, obviously, provides a clear picture about achieving or missing results and about accountability. Hence, the data challenge, often mistaken as a dry and dull exercise for statisticians, has the potential to be an eye-opener and a game-changer.

Taking into account this ongoing work on improving data and measuring, the SDG global indicator framework is refined annually and reviewed comprehensively every five years, i.e., in 2020 and 2025, before the deadline in 2030. With the revision in 2020, the indicator framework was amended to 231 indicators. But nevertheless, they have to stick with the existing goals and targets, as agreed in 2015, with all their flaws and shortcomings. Thus, one of the important lessons learned for future agreements or frameworks is to involve statisticians from the very beginning. For the 2030 Agenda, they were involved rather late in the process, in fact only when member states had basically agreed on the goals and targets.

Finally, there is also a price tag and a heavy workload that comes with the data revolution. If the 8 MDG goals and the 28 targets had been measured in a scientific sound way between 1990 and 2015, this would have cost at least some $27 billion or about $1 billion per target. When applying this to today's SDGs and their 169 targets, the overall price tag jumps to $169 billion (Jerven 2018: 91–94). That is more than two-thirds of the annual total sum spent on Official Development Assistance (ODA), which was $223 billion in 2023. There is a wide range of estimates calculating that measuring the current indicator framework per year would land somewhere between $650 million and $3 billion (Kubiszewski et al. 2021: 140; MacFeely 2020: 368). It certainly would be unacceptable to spend almost as much on the measuring tools as on the substance itself; thus, measuring and monitoring of SDG progress has to become cheaper, simpler and faster. Since the adoption of the SDGs, funding for data and statistics has increased from $591 million in 2015 to $693 million in 2018 but was leveling off the following year (United Nations 2021: 61).

In hindsight, the SDG indicator framework and the subsequent advances in monitoring and measuring were one of the most overlooked and unnoticed great advances that came with the SDGs. Seemingly happening only in the background and mostly satisfying nerds in statistics and science in the first place, the progress in ensuring quality data and measures, despite some flawed and fluffy goals and targets, were an outstanding contribution to enhancing accountability for all parties. The SDGs turned into a driving force for breaking new statistical ground on concepts and methodology but also regarding the use of new data sources (MacFeely 2020: 370–371). There certainly are limits to what can be properly measured and displayed in form of quantifiable data and statistics. Nevertheless, the data topic will make even more headway in the coming years, given the global acceptance and the proven added value of sound and transparent monitoring and measuring. Without doubt, the SDGs were a decisive push for sustainability and sustainability policies to become evidence- and science-based, and to have measurable and comparable results across countries, beyond political interpretation.

Hitting the moving target: About synergies, trade-offs, and wicked sustainability challenges

The MDGs were a comparably simple endeavor: poverty was basically boiled down to some few numbers to define poverty and what needed to be done about it. The end goal of the MDGs was clear: leaving behind poverty in the Global South through emulating the in the Global North prevailing growth model of prosperity. With the SDGs, however, it was very different, as sustainability is much more complex and cannot easily be boiled down to some few numbers. Furthermore, the end goal is not that clear as there is no existing role model to emulate. Identifying the truly sustainable patterns in every part of life is still work in progress. Also, merging the poverty and the environmental agendas and adding the economic dimension, produced extremely complex and tricky challenges about how to reconcile the three at times conflicting dimensions of sustainable development.

Beneath the surface of popular slogans about "going green" are a bunch of so-called wicked problems. Problems are wicked, if the underlying causes are highly uncertain, if the way of solving these is highly contradictory and contentious, and if easy and uncontested solutions are rare. These tend to be not just right or wrong but often something in-between, and require weighing beneficial and detrimental impacts against each other. All of this perfectly applies to the SDGs. Fighting poverty, promoting economic wellbeing and prosperity can easily clash with protecting the environment as these goals are to some extent obviously conflicting. Hence, advancing sustainability means continuously considering and weighing all potential economic, social, or environmental side effects to identify solutions. And usually there are many side effects, and fatally some of them become apparent only many years later.

For example, increasing food production to eliminate hunger appears as the obvious answer, but this easily has backlashes and negative repercussions on other dimensions in the sustainability equation, in this case on the environment, if the answer is to simply intensify or expand agriculture. Agriculture can satisfy people's current need for food, but at the same time have long-term negative impacts on soil, climate, or biodiversity. Fishery can satisfy people's current need for food, but at the same time have long-term negative impacts on fish stocks and subsequently on the ocean's ecosystems. Industry can satisfy people's current need for jobs and cheap everyday products, but at the same time have negative long-term impacts on workers' health or the environment. The same conundrum applies to many material shortcomings, like lack of energy, infrastructure or goods in general, where producing and providing more of what is lacking can easily backfire and lead to devastating environmental or social consequences. Weighing and assessing all potential impacts often leads to decisions full of hard-fought compromises, second-best solutions, and unintended consequences. Going sustainable, in fact, means to identify the best way forward in a given moment, and accepting sustainability as a never-ending, continuously evolving challenge. There is no one and only perfect solution, working all across the world under all conditions.

The MDGs had the advantage of not conveying possibly conflicting messages, or let's say, at the time there was no thorough discussion that fighting poverty could possibly compromise on environmental issues. The SDGs, however, are full of these wicked sustainability problems and bear considerable potential for conflicts. SDG 8 (growth and employment) and SDG 9 (infrastructure and industrialization) are obviously not easily reconcilable with SDG 13 (combating climate change), SDG 14 (protecting the oceans), or SDG 15 (protecting terrestrial ecosystems). In particular, the climate goal appears largely incompatible with a continued GDP growth scenario; many scientific studies call for an almost zero-growth scenario instead.

In fact, there has been much criticism that the forthright call for sustained economic growth has found its way into the SDGs at all. The developing countries had pushed for this goal, stressing the need for poor countries to grow as the only way to effectively fight poverty. Economic growth, indeed, has always been and remains key for eliminating poverty. Experience from the last decades has shown that without large-scale economic growth and industrialization none of the MICs, like China, India, Vietnam, or Brazil, would have managed to end extreme poverty for most of their populations. No country has ever caught up through farming alone, and although in most developing countries the agricultural sector was also expanding, manufacturing and services were decisively leading the way for people leaving behind poverty. The fully sustainable growth model that is equally able to lift millions out of poverty still has to be identified (Manuel et al. 2018: 15–20; Roser/Ortiz-Ospina 2019; World Bank 2024b: 67–68).

Assessing and weighing all potential impacts and identifying the best sustainable way forward easily comes close to squaring the circle as these figures illustrate:

The food sector accounts for roughly one-third of global energy use and for almost one-third of total greenhouse gas emissions. Agriculture takes up nearly 50 percent of all habitable land and 70 percent of freshwater consumption. Increases in food production have led to a steep rise in water and land use, intensive mono-cropping, and intensive use of fertilizers and pesticides. As a result, agriculture has considerably contributed to soil contamination, land degradation, loss of biodiversity as well as destruction of natural habitats. Between 1985 and 2005, 70 percent of the grassland, 50 percent of the savanna, and 27 percent of the tropical forests have been cleared or converted into pastures and croplands. But nevertheless, there is still a lot of hunger in the world, and in some places, food insecurity is even rising. For many years, stepping up high-intensity agriculture appeared as the most effective solution. But with a view to critical ecological thresholds and the environmental impact, solely focusing on crop yields while neglecting soil health or freshwater supplies, is extremely unsustainable. As agriculture in the end depends on a healthy environment, this equals shooting into your own foot. Hence, just producing more food the traditional way is definitely not the solution but rather a conundrum in the wicked sustainability equation still to be solved (Ceres2030 2020: 8–9; Morgan Stanley 2020: 12; UNDESA 2014: 21–26).

There still persists a huge knowledge gap about how a fully sustainable agriculture could function at scale, how to effectively reduce its toll on climate and ecosystems while addressing the remaining hunger. The type of food grown also plays a role. Livestock as a whole is responsible for 14 percent of total global greenhouse gas emissions, with cattle being the most polluting. On average, one kilo of meat produces nearly 13 times more greenhouse gases than one kilo of vegetables. Each calorie of food from livestock on average requires 15 times more land than a calorie directly from crops. Currently, livestock accounts for two-thirds of all land used for agricultural purposes, yet only produces roughly 18 percent of the world's calories (Morgan Stanley 2020: 84–95). The scientists responsible for the Global Sustainable Development Report in 2023, outlined that $4 billion investments in agriculture per year had the potential to nearly end hunger by 2030. But an additional $6.5 billion per year investments in technical climate-smart options would be needed to achieve reducing greenhouse gas emissions consistent with the 1.5 degrees Celsius pathway (United Nations 2023b: 53). The Ceres2030 Study, a multidisciplinary team report by the International Food Policy Research Institute, similarly calculated that almost $14 billion per year on average would be needed to not just end hunger but do this in line with the Paris Climate Agreement (Laborde et al. 2020: 23–24).

A very telling example from the agricultural sector about how difficult it is to find truly sustainable solutions is palm oil. Once hailed for being a cheap but natural product, oil palm trees turned into a threat for tropical forests and natural habitats. Since the 1990s, the land used for palm oil production has almost quadrupled, from 6 million in 1990 to a peak of 20 million hectares in 2015, and declining since then. In particular between 2005 and 2015, oil palm plantations were the largest driver of deforestation in Indonesia, providing more than half of the world production, and Malaysia, providing roughly a quarter. There has never been a produce that so quickly morphed from bliss into disaster, heartbreakingly pictured by the orangutans that lost their homes due to the swathes of cleared rainforest to grow oil palm trees.

Does that mean that palm oil is an unsustainable crop that needs to be banned? Rather not, as this question is a lot more complex. There are several reasons why palm oil was the favored crop to respond to the steep rise in global demand for vegetable oils: first, low production costs, second, its versatility as it can be used for food and non-food purposes alike, and third, unmatched high yields. One hectare of land can produce 2.8 tons of palm oil. That is around four times more than alternatives produce, such as sunflower or rapeseed oil (producing 0.7 tons per hectare respectively). Grown only in the tropics, palm oil was also seen as a good source of stable income for farmers in tropical developing countries.

The world uses altogether 300 million hectares for oil crop production. Palm oil accounts for only 6 percent of the used land while producing 36 percent of the global amount of vegetable oils, due to its high yields. The second popular oil crop, soybean, takes up 39 percent of the global land use for vegetable oil production, while accounting for 25 percent of the global vegetable oil production. Switching to alternatives to palm oil would mean using much more land for growing oil crops, with all environmental implications included. Hence, banning palm oil is obviously not the solution. Instead, many stakeholders started engaging in identifying sustainable solutions,[15] like certification schemes as developed by the Roundtable on Sustainable Palm Oil (RSPO).[16] These aim at ensuring that palm oil is produced under strict sustainability requirements, such as impact assessments, biodiversity and tropical forest management, and avoidance of land clearance (Ritchie/Roser 2021).

In the case of food and agriculture, the wicked sustainability challenges and potential trade-offs lie in reconciling SDG 1 (ending poverty) and SDG 2 (ending hunger, achieving food security) with SDG 13 (combating climate change), SDG 14 (protecting the oceans), and SDG 15 (protecting terrestrial ecosystems). In this regard, target 2.4 is quite comprehensive and entails most of the relevant aspects:

> By 2030, ensure sustainable food production systems and implement resilient agricultural practices that increase productivity and production, that help maintain ecosystems, that strengthen capacity for adaptation to climate change, extreme weather, drought, flooding and other disasters and that progressively improve land and soil quality.

Leaving aside that this is another overloaded target, it describes pretty well what it takes to make agriculture truly sustainable. How this can be achieved in real life, however, is a conundrum in the wicked sustainability equation still to be solved.

A very different but equally revealing example for wicked sustainability challenges is energy that can result in both tremendous social and economic benefits as well as devastating environmental impacts. Just providing simple things, such as light, power, heating, and cooling have proven to be invaluable enablers for poor children benefiting from better education and being healthier, and poor people benefiting from more opportunities for jobs and income generation. But there are still 790 million people without access to electricity, and 2.6 billion people with no clean cooking options.

However, if energy continues being provided in a traditional rampant greenhouse gas-emitting way, it will wreak havoc on the climate and ecosystems beyond repair. Between 2000 and 2020, globally the proportion of population with access to electricity rose from 78 to 90 percent. At the same time, greenhouse gas emissions from electricity and heating rose from 1.7 to 1.9 tons per capita. The energy sector is the source of around three-quarters of greenhouse gas emissions and, thus, a major contributor to climate change and its subsequent impacts. Also, according to the World Health Organization, air pollution is leading to over 6 million premature deaths worldwide per year through heart and lung diseases, stroke, or cancer. Around 90 percent of those premature deaths occur in low- and middle-income countries.[17]

Studies have analyzed the potential impact of ending poverty on reducing greenhouse gas emissions. As emissions from households in extreme poverty are minimal anyway, moving these out of extreme poverty, unsurprisingly, would have only a minimal effect with 4.7 percent more CO_2 emissions. However, these numbers change considerably when calculating the potential impact of moving the more numerous poor people in middle-income countries over the MIC poverty line of $6.85 per day. This would lead to an extraordinary increase of CO_2 emissions by 46 percent. Very obviously, expanding energy access as quickly as possible in an affordable and easily accessible way to the poor can only be sustainable, if concurrently a transitioning toward renewable energy takes place to not counteract the climate commitments (World Bank 2024b: 183–185).

In the quest for clean energy, solar and wind energy appear as near-perfect sustainable solutions. However, also solar and wind energy have environmental impacts. If solar and wind, which could easily triple until 2040 and provide between 12 and 26 percent of global power, were to become the primary sources of energy based on current technologies, this would subsequently lead to fatal mineral resource exploitation. In a scenario that meets the Paris climate goals, a four to six times general increase in mineral demand would be the consequence. The demand for lithium, graphite, nickel, and cobalt as well as rare earths is projected to skyrocket 42 times, 25 times, 19 times, 21 times, and 7 times, respectively, by 2040, in particular needed for grid storage and batteries (IEA 2021b: 21; Newell et al. 2020: 12). As these minerals are not renewable, current renewable energy systems could experience supply shortages and price spikes, and, hence, require much more innovation to keep on functioning in the long run.

Also, mining for critical minerals usually is water- and energy-intensive, and many minerals are located in areas that already suffer from high water stress. There are estimates that achieving net-zero CO_2 emissions with clean energy would lead to roughly twice the land and water demand compared to fossil fuel energy systems. And regarding deep-sea mining, there are still many scientific unknowns about the effects on marine life and the ocean environment. In addition, some of the top providers of minerals are conflict-affected countries which often provokes human rights and child labor issues (UNEP 2024b: 13–18).

Another often ignored unsustainable aspect are the still infant recycling capacities. IRENA anticipates a steep global rise of discarded solar panels, reaching between 2 and 8 million tons by 2030 and skyrocketing to 60–78 million tons by 2050. In this scenario, China alone could be throwing out up to 20 million tons of solar panels by 2050, followed by India with 19 million and the US with 10 million (IRENA 2016: 32–35). Other researchers project even 50 times more discarded solar panels from the 2030s on as innovation could accelerate replacement cycles. This solar trash deluge could lead to the volume of waste surpassing that of new installations by the year 2031. An estimated cost of $20–30 to recycle one panel today compared to $1–2 for sending a panel to a landfill, indicates clearly the looming threat of a solar trash mountain. Similar scenarios loom for the wind energy industry with more than 720,000 tons of gargantuan wind-turbine blades expected to end up in US landfills over the next 20 years (Atasu et al. 2021; Holger 2022; IRENA 2016: 12–13; Lopes 2024).

These examples underscore that eliminating one negative impact, in this case CO_2 emissions, can only be fully sustainable, if alternative solutions consider thoroughly their overall economic, social, and environmental impacts. Hence, for solar and wind energy systems to be fully sustainable, much more research and, certainly, regulation is needed for improving recycling, refurbishing and reusing, as well as material substitution. The same applies to batteries and storage systems where recycling and repairing remains rather difficult (UNEP 2024b: 25). The industry still has a long way to go. And of all sectors, green technologies can afford the least to not incorporate the full impacts of its products and services into the sustainability equation.

In the case of energy, the wicked sustainability challenges and potential trade-offs lie in reconciling SDG 7 (energy), SDG 8 (growth and employment) and SDG 9 (infrastructure and industrialization) with SDG 12 (sustainable consumption and production), SDG 13 (combating climate change), SDG 14 (protecting the oceans), and SDG 15 (protecting terrestrial ecosystems). What truly sustainable energy solutions look like and how they can be implemented, is a conundrum in the wicked sustainability equation still to be solved.

The interlinkages between the SDGs offer much potential for both trade-offs as well as synergies. Since a couple of years, there is more and more research being done on identifying the nature and scope of those trade-offs and synergies and how to effectively trigger progress on various goals at the same time. Many studies are outlining that the synergies in general outweigh the potential trade-offs, that the chances to achieve several goals simultaneously through targeted action is bigger than making progress on one goal at the expense of another. The environmental SDGs 14 on oceans and 15 on ecosystems are clearly the most negatively affected by progress in other areas. Other SDGs, like 4 on education, 5 on gender equality, 6 on water, or 17 on partnerships are clearly associated with producing considerable concurrent progress on several other goals (Bennich et al. 2023: 1465–1466; United Nations 2023b: 33–36; van Vuuren et al. 2022). There is a plethora of tools available to support countries in unlocking as many synergies as possible and managing potential trade-offs, such as SDG Synergies,[18] Enabling SDGs,[19] the Sustainable Development Simulator,[20] modeling the long-term consequences of policies, or the SDG Climate Action Nexus tool,[21] providing guidance on the impact of climate action on achieving the SDGs. But much more research is needed to better understand how to manage SDG interlinkages in practice, and how they relate to specific local issues and contexts to accelerate progress (Bennich et al. 2023: 1471–1473).

Going sustainable, in fact, means to hit the moving target. Fully sustainable solutions for many present-day challenges are still being searched for, technologies are still evolving and many dominant technology solutions have yet to emerge. Thus, science and innovation play a crucial role in the quest for sustainability. Also, something that is the latest sustainable solution today could already be outdated some years later because of new scientific findings or innovation. The One Vanderbuilt skyscraper in the heart of Manhattan, supposed to be an environmental marvel and a new standard in green buildings, experienced this fate. Many green features that were the right climate and energy solutions in 2016 when the works started, were already outdated by 2020 when the building opened. A rapidly evolving energy-policy landscape and standards can overtake the best intentions and ambitious projects in sustainability in only a few years (Howe 2023).

How much there is still unknown about going sustainable is underscored by some projections. The International Energy Agency (IEA) estimates that by 2050 half of the CO_2 reductions will come from technologies that are currently at the demonstration or prototype phase. A big boost in research and innovation is needed for a thorough transformation in the energy sector, spurring systemic transition to low-carbon, green energies. It is possible that by 2050 electricity generation from zero-carbon technologies grows faster than demand, but this is largely depending on the costs, reliability, and availability of the respective technologies and how much policies pave the way for them (Galiana 2018: 149–162; EIA 2023: 31–36; IEA 2021a: 14–18, 2021b: 167–179).

Searching for sustainable solutions, in fact, means managing and weighing a myriad of practical and economic factors. This has to come with the humility to recognize that there is still so much that needs to be learned and understood about human interaction with nature and the impacts on the environment, about the assimilative and regenerative capacities of ecosystems and what really is sustainable. Solutions and approaches have to be constantly critically analyzed and assessed against their possible knock-on effects on the environment, on human wellbeing, or other realms of life. Likewise, potential pathways for going sustainable have to be dynamic and learn in continuous feedback loops about what is working and what is moving the needle in the right direction, as everything humans do has an impact on the earth's ecosystems. There is, in fact, no greater challenge for humanity than finding sustainable ways of living and working without backsliding into preindustrial poverty.

The 2030 Agenda entails most of those wicked challenges of sustainability but, of course, does not provide detailed answers on how to reconcile more food, more economic prosperity, and employment for more people with reducing the human footprint and protecting the environment, let alone operational plans. No one expected the 2030 Agenda to provide that, and no one of those involved in devising the SDGs ever had the ambition to do that. The 2030 Agenda, in fact, provides the titles and the cues, showing the way and the direction, but leaves many blank spaces in between, with much room to decide what to do and how to do it. Those dealing with everyday questions about how to manage agriculture, industry, urbanization, energy, etc. in a sustainable but still affordable and just way, have to walk the talk and put the SDGs into action.

Governments, politicians, and other actors are facing major predicaments and tough choices, in particular when it comes to questions of how to reconcile reducing the environmental footprint with economic growth. While eliminating poverty is an uncontested social good and moral obligation that is expected to produce winners only, sustainable development is a much more convoluted and complex concept, easily stirring suspicion and wariness that some might be winning while others might be losing. Discussions about shutting down coal plants and other cheap energy providers, reducing air travel, restricting the use of cheap but polluting material or other conveniences show that not everyone embraces a sustainability agenda as openly and full-heartedly as a poverty agenda. No one wants to seriously propose lowering living standards or economic activity, reducing convenience in products and services or too much authoritative interfering in consumers' choices and the markets. And in emerging economies, where many people are enjoying economic opportunities, the generation before could only dream of, who would dare denying them these amenities and comforts?

Furthermore, the temptation to look for a "free ride" in climate and environmental action, nudging others to make sacrifices from which all will benefit, is high. In addition, questions of prices, access, or potential side effects can easily render a theoretical solution not feasible in real life. The cost of an innovation or a cultural or social aspect of a policy can be a stumbling block as the most sustainable solution is not necessarily the most cost-efficient one or socially acceptable. And, regrettably, the consequences of inaction in environmental issues will be felt only many years later. For good or bad, tackling sustainability issues is often left to the whims of elected politicians caring more about canvassing voters and catering to their economic wellbeing in the short term than ensuring healthy and sustainable economies and ecosystems in the long term (McNeill/Engelke 2014: 80; Pradhan et al. 2017: 1173–1174; Svizzero/Tisdell 2015: 15–22; UNEP 2024b: 30–32).

However, even if all solutions for those wicked and complex sustainability challenges were available and uncontested, and if there was broad willingness to implement them, achieving all SDGs by 2030 still would require a revolutionary transformation of human life on earth at almost utopian speed and scale. The MDGs, fighting hunger and the worst destitutions on earth, already appeared as a humongous task. But the SDGs with their all-encompassing character and wicked sustainability challenges, lacking easy uncontested success formulas and models to emulate, appear as a task for at least a generation.

The business case for sustainability: Are the SDGs reconciling profit and purpose?

In January 2016, something remarkable happened: only four months after the adoption of the 2030 Agenda, the world's business leaders, coming together at the annual World Economic Forum in Davos, discussed the economic benefits and the business opportunities of sustainable development and how the private sector could contribute to achieving the SDGs. Until then, the UN and the business world had a rather awkward and uneasy relationship: the latter was only very little interested in UN processes as these were largely perceived as governments' business, mostly dealing with peace and security, or fighting poverty. And the UN had been rather warily gazing at the private sector as a world that hardly cared about anything beyond increasing the return on investment.

However, in the post-2015 process, unusual for UN negotiations, business representatives were involved from the very beginning as the UN was ready to change its relationship with the business world. And Unilever, DuPont, and many more companies didn't want to be rubberstamped any more as being part of the problem but as being part of the solution. During the MDG era, the private sector was mostly seen as an opponent whose influence and dominance had to be curbed, in particular its supposed mostly detrimental repercussions on international efforts to fight poverty. The same applied to the environmental agenda; the private sector was the perpetrator and polluter that had to be submitted to strict control. Profit and purpose were perceived to be at odds with each other; doing good was seen as something for the donor community, NGOs, and philanthropists that would cost money and was not in line with the traditional shareholder-value approach. But since a couple of years, this thinking has been changing at breathtaking speed. And the 2030 Agenda clearly added its two cents to this development.

But incorporating the economic dimension into the SDGs was quite fraught with controversy, often producing second-best compromises. During the post-2015 negotiations, there was much debate about how much growth was needed to eliminate poverty and foster prosperity and wellbeing, what kind of growth was needed to make it sustainable and who would be the actors turning the tide and making unsustainable growth sustainable. In the end, the goals eventually explicitly addressing the economic dimension, SDG 7 (energy), SDG 8 (growth and employment), SDG 9 (infrastructure and industrialization), and SDG 12 (consumption and production), reflected these controversies. They were addressing many new issues, but concurrently repeating many rather unsustainable tenets from traditional economic thinking. The caveat about incorporating GDP growth into SDG 8 as a rather old-fashioned measure for prosperity, not taking into account sustainability aspects, has already been discussed in this chapter. However, the target on decoupling economic growth from environmental degradation gave the goal a transformative twist toward sustainability. Similarly, SDG 9 with the targets on more infrastructure and more industrialization, like economic growth also pushed by developing countries, were clearly lacking a transformative character. However, the targets on scientific research and innovation gave the goal a twist to look beyond existing models and invest in progress.

SDG 7 on affordable, reliable, sustainable, and modern energy is obviously one of the key goals, reflecting the already outlined conundrum between expanding energy access as quickly as possible while at the same time transitioning toward renewable energy. But so far, the results are something between mixed and sobering. The good news is that the energy transition is well under way; change is happening at a breathtaking pace and going beyond any initial expectations. Between 2010 and 2023, solar photovoltaic capacity has increased 35-fold, and wind energy 4-fold. Renewables have become compellingly competitive and more cost-efficient than fossil fuels. Since 2000, the cost of solar photovoltaic has plunged by almost 90 percent and of onshore wind energy by almost 70 percent. The renewable power deployed since 2000, in 2023 globally had saved an estimated $409 billion in fuel costs in the electricity sector alone (IRENA 2024: 14–20). In 2023, global annual investments in renewables reached a new record with $658 billion which is almost double the investment of $331 billion in 2015. Solar was the key driver in this astonishing development. However, this investment boom in renewables is eclipsing the poorest countries. At current rates, LDCs would need almost 40 years to catch up with the average level of renewable energy installment in developing countries. Political instabilities and a lacking regulatory environment in LDCs are pushing up the cost of capital and hampering any transformative development at scale (Malcomson 2020; United Nations, Inter-agency Task Force on Financing for Development 2024: 38).

But despite this considerable pace of change, the bad news is that this is by far not enough to reach a net-zero 2050 scenario and, thus, achieve the Paris climate goals and the SDGs. Limiting global warming below 1.5 degrees requires emissions to decline by 80 percent in developed economies, by 60 percent in middle-income and developing countries by 2035 compared with the 2022 level. And this looks extremely unlikely

(IEA et al. 2024: 129; United Nations 2024: 35; UN High-Level Expert Group 2022: 23–24; World Bank 2024b: 181–182).

At the same time, fossil fuels continue playing a significant role. The share of fossil fuels in the global energy mix has only come down very slowly from 82 percent in 2013 to 80 percent in 2023. In 2021, governments spent an estimated $722 billion on subsidizing coal, oil and gas, and in 2022, global subsidies jumped to a shocking record of $1.5 trillion. This surge is broadly the consequence of the war in Ukraine. Although intended to support vulnerable households, subsidies often disproportionately benefit wealthier people and carbon-intensive industries. In 2022, Russia was the largest single provider of fossil fuel subsidies, followed by Iran and China.[22] The billions in fossil fuel subsidies are in striking contradiction to their envisaged phasing out as stipulated in target 12.c and are clearly undermining efforts to combat climate change. Obviously, vested interests are hampering transformative change and investments in sustainable technologies (IEA 2024: 24; Sachs et al. 2024: 4).

At current pace, so far, the energy SDG and its targets remain out of reach. In 2021, the global share in renewables in the total energy mix was at just 18.7 percent, only a few percentages higher than in 2010, and is projected to land somewhere between 18 and 23 percent by 2030. The pledge by more than 130 countries at the COP28 in Dubai in 2023 to triple renewable capacity by 2030 is possible, but requires much more commitment, targeted policy interventions and, most of all, investment at scale. Clean power generation would have to double globally, and solar and wind energy alone would have to increase by 60–70 percent. Energy is, in fact, the SDG with the largest investment gap, followed by water and sanitation and infrastructure. Since 2015, investment in clean energy has increased by 60 percent, but for net-zero it would have to double until 2035. That means an estimated $1 trillion of annual investment into clean energy would be needed in developing countries alone to achieve net-zero by 2050, and $3–5 trillion annual investments would be needed globally (IEA 2024: 61–66; IEA et al. 2024: 13–16, 107; UN High-Level Expert Group 2022: 30–33; United Nations, Inter-agency Task Force on Financing for Development 2024: 72).

Concurrently and sadly, about 660 million people, that is 8 percent of the global population, are likely to remain without electricity by 2030, 85 percent of them in Sub-Sahara Africa. There, the share of the population with electricity access has barely increased in a decade due to population growth. Thus, very likely, also the target on universal energy access will be clearly missed (IEA 2024: 55–57; United Nations 2023a: 26–27).

SDG 8, besides promoting growth, also entails the challenge of the century: decoupling economic growth from an overuse of resources, as delineated in target 8.4 ("improve ... global resource efficiency in consumption and production and endeavour to decouple economic growth from environmental degradation"). But so far, overshooting and depleting of resources is further on the rise with no reversing of this trend in sight, much to the contrary. A sustainable level of resource use is estimated at about 50 billion metric tons per year – a boundary that was breached in 2000 and since then regularly overshot, as the Global Footprint Network[23] is sounding the alarm bells each year. Globally, between 2000 and 2017, the overall material footprint increased by 70 percent. In particular, MICs had a significantly higher impact in the past two decades, due to rapid industrialization and strong economic growth. If this kind of resource use continues, material extraction is set to increase to a very unsustainable 140 billion tons annually by 2050 (EIA 2021: 4; UNDESA 2014: 73–82, 168; United Nations 2021: 50–51).

Decoupling, in fact, boils down to the question whether innovation can outrun depletion and produce enough and effective substitutes for the various minerals, fuels, and natural resources that human activities depend on. Scenarios of depleting and draining resources loom at the horizon, and their impact could be terrible, even grind human activity to a halt. Scientific evidence suggests that absolute decoupling within the timespan of the SDGs is extremely unlikely. The only way to avoid ecological collapse, scientists conclude, is to impose hard caps on resource use, ensuring that not more is extracted from the land and the seas than the earth can safely regenerate. But even improved technologies and innovations can hardly compensate for misguided behavioral patterns, such as overconsumption or a single-use mentality and unsustainable human activities (Bonnedahl et al. 2022: 151–152; Eisenmenger et al. 2020: 1106–1108; Hickel 2018, 2019).

Science and research underscore that decoupling, in fact, means moving toward a circular economy. In a circular economy, products and materials are designed in a way that they can be reused, remanufactured, recycled, or recovered, so that the single components remain in the economy as long as possible. This would significantly reduce or minimize the material footprint and greenhouse gas emissions. As currently only less than 10 percent of all waste are globally recycled back into productive circles of the economy, there is a lot of room for improving circularity practices (McDonough/Braungart 2013: 123–168; Raworth 2017: 221; UNEP 2024a: 36). Picturing a sustainable economy as a "doughnut economy" illustrates where to draw the boundaries. The doughnut's inner ring sets out the safe realm for a decent living and human well-being. The doughnut's outer ring delineates the ecological boundaries what nature can sustain. Overstepping them means draining natural resources, extinction of biological diversity, pollution, and irreversible environmental degradation. These must be the clear limits for all human activity (Raworth 2017: 45). The SDGs, however, don't mention circular economic models, which is a clear shortcoming, but at least measure waste, recycling rates and tons of recycled material.

So far, achieving SDG 8 remains out of reach as the growth, productivity, and employment targets suffer from a general global economic slowdown, and reducing resource use and decoupling are far from any progress.

Companies are only explicitly addressed by SDG 12 on sustainable consumption and production, in target 12.6 ("encourage companies, especially large and transnational companies, to adopt sustainable practices and to integrate sustainability information into their reporting cycle"). Considering the key role of the business world in going sustainable, this is blatantly unambitious. Nevertheless, many individual businesses and associations have taken action as they realize that low performance in environmental, social, and governance criteria could pose risks to their long-term business as well as brands and reputation. More and more companies are disclosing non-financial aspects of their operations, such as carbon emissions, use of natural resources or social indicators like gender equity in pay and benefit or diversity of staff (Williams et al. 2023). Reporting on environmental, social, and governance factors (ESG) is booming. In 2011, only 20 percent of the S&P 500 companies published sustainability reports, in 2017 already 85 percent did so, and in 2022 the number had risen to 98 percent.[24] The number of ESG or sustainability indexes around the world has equally mushroomed from less than 10 in 1993 to almost 500 in 2016 and more than 1,000 in 2020 (UNCTAD 2021: 218–219).

There is a profusion of initiatives, like the Global Reporting Initiative[25] or the International Sustainability Standards Board,[26] established at the COP26 in 2021, that are giving valuable guidance. But so far, reporting is only voluntary, and some apply quite high sustainability standards, while others provide rather meaningless information. However, as long as there are no common reporting standards, ESG or other sustainability reports are rather difficult to compare. Common criteria regarding the ecological footprint, greenhouse gas emissions, or the general sustainability performance of a company are clearly missing (BlackRock 2019; United Nations, Inter-agency Task Force on Financing for Development 2020: 75; UN High-Level Expert Group 2022: 28–29).

Subsequently, there is a high risk of so-called "greenwashing" or "SDG-washing", i.e., window-dressing actions that are overstating the green impact and making misleading assertions about going sustainable (Williams et al. 2023). This regulatory gap is only slowly being closed. The EU, for example, introduced a Corporate Sustainability Reporting Directive,[27] in force since 2023, that is demanding from companies to disclose their sustainability-related impacts and provide specific comparable data on their sustainability performance. Regulators are also increasingly stepping up the fight against misleading information on sustainability and are cracking down on greenwashing. An increasing number of companies are being sued for inflating their sustainability performance. Prominent cases are multiplying, such as the UK Advertising Standards Authority (ASA) banning ads from HSBC or Ryanair in 2023 (Bothello et al. 2023).

While SDG 8 covers the transformation of economies in general, SDG 12 breaks the economic dimension down to some key areas, supporting the general decoupling aims, in particular target 12.2 ("achieve the sustainable management and efficient use of natural resources"), target 12.3 ("halve per capita global food waste"), target 12.5 ("substantially reduce waste generation through prevention, reduction, recycling and reuse") but also target 9.4 ("upgrade infrastructure and retrofit industries to make them sustainable, with increased resource use efficiency") as well as target 11.6 ("reduce the adverse per capita environmental impact of cities").

In particular for the targets on reducing resource use and waste, the projections are quite worrying. Increasing extraction rates of natural resources, leads to them being fed into unsustainable linear economic models and eventually ending up as mountains of waste, often toxic and not degradable. If no urgent action is taken, global municipal waste, excluding industrial waste and construction debris, is projected to increase from 2.1 billion tons in 2020 to 3.7 billion tons by 2050. By far the strongest increase of waste is projected to be generated in the fast-growing economies in East and South-East Asia with North America ranking second in waste increase. In 2020, almost 40 percent of all waste was just dumped somewhere or burned in the open, less than one-third ended up in landfills and only less than one-third was reused or recycled. And sadly, more than half of global waste consisted of food, which leaves the world painfully off track from the target of halving global food waste (UNEP 2024a: 18–21).

One of the most intractable challenges is the fatally flawed and unsustainable use of supposedly free or cheap resources and natural ecosystems. Cheap plastic, for example, and other cheap products are, in fact, only cheap because the externalities are not priced in, that is the use of clean air and water, and of ecosystems exposed to waste and residues. Each year, over 400 million tons of plastic are produced, and around 8 million tons are reaching the rivers and oceans. That means globally the amount of one garbage truck of plastic is dumped into the ocean every minute. Over time, 10 billion tons of plastic have been produced, of which an estimated 6 billion ended up in landfills or somewhere in open nature. Globally, only 9 percent of plastic waste is recycled. Without regulatory change, plastic demand is projected to double until 2050 and even triple until 2100. And, very scarily, if the rate of plastic waste ending up in the oceans continues at this scale, by 2050 plastic in the ocean might even outweigh fish (EIA 2021: 4; Parker 2024; Ritchie et al. 2023).

Assessing the true value of ecosystem services is a most complex calculation. The price tag is reaching something between $30 trillion and more than $100 trillion (e.g., IPCC 2019; The White House, Office of Information and Regulatory Affairs 2023; United Nations et al. 2021). If priced in, single-use and products with toxic ingredients would not be cheap anymore, and subsequently, markets, prices, and consumer habits would change. In this scenario, business-as-usual and traditional growth, leading to depleting natural resources, should be extremely expensive. A sustainable economy is largely incompatible with business being allowed to outsource responsibility for the earth's ecosystems and to insource economic benefits (Herrington 2021; Jackson 2017: 12–17).

Disappointingly, there is a growing gap between "green" promises and real action. In 2023, there was a 40 percent increase of Forbes Global 2000 companies, the largest companies in the world, pledging to become net-zero. Yet, many of them fail to take the needed action to advance on their promises. And many businesses still have no net-zero or sustainability pledges at all. Furthermore, there is a worryingly high number of companies using all means to dodge strict environmental regulations, to cover up their supply chains, or to make use of regulation loopholes or of regulators prone to bribery. Meanwhile, others are genuinely interested in changing their business models, either seeing the economic opportunities of venturing to new markets or seeing a moral obligation toward the earth or a mix of both. In the end, going sustainable has to pay off, and it has to happen on a level playing field, otherwise it's not going to work.

There are many inspiring initiatives in the business world, such as "Race to Zero,"[28] the "Net-Zero Asset Owner Alliance,"[29] the "Breakthrough Energy Network,"[30] the "First Movers Coalition",[31] or the "Zero Hunger Private Sector Pledge."[32] The World Benchmarking

Alliance,[33] pushing for one global accountability mechanism, identified the 2,000 most influential global companies (SDG2000) and assessed and ranked their commitments and achievements in sustainability. But these initiatives are coalitions of the willing and are unlikely to alter corporate behavior sufficiently. The business world has to move beyond the pioneers, and sustainability criteria have to be embedded into the core business strategies and practices of every business, ranking equally alongside financial and operational goals (Nelson 2018: 102).

In the end, governments have a pivotal role in ensuring that laggards are being held accountable and leaders being recognized for the investments and the risks they take. They have to set ambitious targets for efficiency and circularity, to incentivize innovation, and to demand responsibility for sustainability. Industry needs to be pushed toward phasing out toxic, harmful components and polluting processes, while phasing in eco-friendly, non-hazardous substances. The level of policy ambition will determine the private sector's response, as companies are much more likely to modify their practices, if they are convinced that governments will take the steadfast lead and commit public interventions to realign private incentives for the cause of sustainability (IEA 2024: 85–87; Jackson 2017: 159–184; Raworth 2017: 237–238; United Nations, Inter-agency Task Force on Financing for Development 2020: 71–72).

One primary example underscoring the importance of the right policy framework is carbon pricing. Carbon pricing is a policy tool to lower CO_2 emissions by creating an economic incentive to shift away from fossil fuels and invest in clean technologies. By 2024, 25 percent of global emissions were under some type of carbon-pricing mechanism. However, the experiences are rather mixed and rocky. In the UK, carbon emissions have drastically fallen because of an effective carbon tax. Canada has one of the most ambitious carbon-pricing mechanisms but is concurrently shielding key industries such as steel and chemicals from a too heavy tax burden. In France and Australia, governments backed down from raising energy costs as they met a fierce backlash and angry street protests (Plumer/Popovich 2019).

Hence, while three-quarters of global emissions still remain unaccounted, carbon pricing often is too modest and too soft to turn the tide in carbon emissions fast enough. In addition, the bulk of climate financing stays in the country of origin, as there is no international carbon market. But carbon credit markets have considerable potential to mobilize substantial resources from the private sector and enable LICs to access climate financing without raising debt. As many developing countries provide most of the carbon assets, this would be a win–win for all (Songwe 2023: 124–125). However, as long as there are pervasive fossil fuel subsidies, their reverse effect on carbon pricing is most likely to render any regulation rather ineffective (World Bank 2024b: 24).

Progress on the economic dimension of sustainable development, is basically boiling down to two aspects: the right policies and the right regulatory framework, and mobilizing financing and investment. The Addis negotiations in July 2015 already gave a foretaste of the enormous financing needs for the SDGs. The World Bank/IMF report "From Billions to Trillions" was emphatically underscoring the major role of the private sector in this as, obviously, the trillions were extremely unlikely to come from public coffers.

Since then, the world of green financing and investing has been growing at an astonishing rate. Sustainable bonds in general, comprising green, social, and mixed-sustainability bonds, are increasingly popular with average annual growth rates of 67 percent, reaching $1.5 trillion in 2020. There are several initiatives, like the Principles for Responsible Investment (PRI),[34] established by the UN already in 2006, that issue recommendations for incorporating ESG criteria into investment practices. Since then, many issuers are further developing criteria under the umbrella of the Green Bond Principles.[35] The Global Investors for Sustainable Development Alliance, set up in 2019, also aims at facilitating financing and long-term investment.[36] But still, going sustainable is shaped by a general lingering wariness whether investors have to forego some financial gains for social and environmental benefits. In the end, it's a lack of agreed criteria and standardization that is hampering trust and ambition (Hestad 2021: 6).

Despite a growing appetite of investors for financing green and sustainable businesses, it's still only a fraction of what would be needed to ignite the envisaged economic transformation of the SDGs. The sustainable bond market is still in its infancy, representing only about 1.24 percent of the total global bond market of approximately $119 trillion. Also, the bulk of these investments goes into developed economies with only a tiny part reaching developing countries (BlackRock 2019; UNCTAD 2021: 208–217; United Nations, Inter-agency Task Force on Financing for Development 2020: 61; World Bank 2024a).

Particularly disadvantaged are low-income and lower-middle-income countries. The COVID-19 pandemic did nothing but exacerbate their situation, producing increasing financing needs while economic growth further slowed down. Thus, in 2022, the number of LICs in financial distress had doubled compared to 2015, and accessing new capital is increasingly difficult. That means in these countries most development advances are rather suffocated, and any SDG progress looks very unlikely

(Kharas/Rivard 2023: 116–118; Sachs et al. 2024: 2–5). The current global financial architecture is not supportive enough of low-income and lower-middle-income countries. The New Global Financing Pact[37] from June 2023 aims at reforming the financial system and, thus, enable all countries, notably the poor, to access more long-term public and private funding.

The pledge of the Addis Agenda from 2015 remains largely unfulfilled, and the billions to trillions, so far, are not pouring in fast enough and targeted enough. Even when calculating all financial flows, DAC- and non-DAC public, multilateral, and private, the picture is rather bleak, and development finance flows have been relatively flat since the SDGs were adopted (Kharas/Rivard 2023: 114–115). Without massively scaling up affordable, long-term financing, there are only slim chances of achieving the SDGs. The pledge of $100 billion climate finance per annum by 2020 was met for the first time in 2022. But again, this is by far not enough. Precisely, the UN sets the amount of funding missing for developing countries alone at $4–6 trillion a year. Achieving all SDGs everywhere is estimated to require $5–7 trillion a year. While this looks like a dwindling amount of money, it still pales in comparison to the costs of inaction. The costs incurred from climate change alone under a business-as-usual scenario through 2050 are estimated to be almost five times larger than the climate finance needed to limit temperature rises to 1.5 degrees Celsius. And to put those estimates into perspective: mobilizing 7.76 percent of global assets under management a year, which is less than the capital exchanged on a single day on the world's financial markets, would suffice to achieve the SDGs. Basically, it's a question of redirecting capital for the cause of sustainability (IPCC 2023; United Nations 2024: 34; United Nations, Inter-agency Task Force on Financing for Development 2024: 2–9, 69).

Finally, a sustainable economic transformation will not be achieved by policies alone. It's the many choices that people are taking in daily life that make a difference. Corporations don't set the pace on social or environmental issues; they rather take their cues from below, from consumers. Thus, societal norms and personal choices play a pivotal role in steering economies onto a sustainable path (Morgan Stanley 2020: 77; Sanwal 2015: 35–36). An increasing number of consumers are wishing to not do any harm with their purchases or even wishing to do good. Once considered a "nice-to-have," sustainability is increasingly guiding consumers' choices between competitors. In particular with younger generations, sustainability has a driving power in buying decisions (Deloitte 2023; Reichheld et al. 2023).

With the SDGs, the private sector and the sustainability agenda have acknowledged their mutual interdependencies and interlinkages. There is no denying that the private sector has a key role in advancing sustainable development through innovation and investment by profit-driven ventures. Some astonishing developments and inspiring initiatives have seen the day of light and keep on reshaping the business world since the SDGs were brought into this world. However, it is by far not enough to reconcile profit and purpose and to ensure economic activities will be nudged into the safe zone of living and working within planetary boundaries.

It's a patchy SDG landscape: Some catch-up on the fast lane, some remain mired in poverty, and the urgency to act is increasing

Before the SDG era, the traditional aid system was characterized by a clear distinction between the countries that were in need, and thus were receiving funding and guidance, and the countries that were able and ready to give, and thus were providing funding and guidance. But with the MDG era coming to an end, the world had changed considerably. The once clear two-polar system with a sharp dividing line between donors and recipients had almost inadvertently morphed into a multi-polar patchy world with different shades of development realities. Recipient countries were overtaking donor countries in economic development and GDP growth, with some of them having turned into both donors and recipients at the same time. Others, however, remained stuck in repeating cycles of poverty, conflict, and misery.

It was, in fact, the rise of the MICs that had upended much of the development world. They had become the new engines of global growth, lifting millions out of poverty, and creating a new middle class. The MICs themselves are quite a diverse group regarding size, economy, growth and income levels, and natural resources. According to the World Bank, MICs are defined as having a per capita Gross National Income (GNI) of $1,136 to $13,845, while LICs are defined by a per capita GNI of $1,135 or less (2022).[38] In the late 1990s, some 63 countries were LICs, representing 59 percent of the world's population and contributing close to 20 percent of the aggregated world GDP (measured in Purchasing Power Parities – PPP). In 2010, only 35 countries were LICs, representing 11 percent of the global population and a minuscule 1.3 percent of global GDP (in PPP). The others had managed to climb up the ladder to some middle-income status. Today, more than half of the world's countries fall under some middle-income classification. From the 1990s to the 2020s, the MICs increased their share in world population from 25 to 75 percent, and their contribution to world GDP rose from 23 to 44 percent. China's share alone of global GDP grew from 2 to 11 percent. Meanwhile, the OECD's share of global GDP fell from 84 percent in 1992 to 64 percent in 2012 (Alonso 2012: 20–22).

The rise of the MICs and the expansion of the global middle class went together with remarkable development progress. In Ethiopia, India, Indonesia, Vietnam, China, and Ghana, for example, more than half of the population lived in extreme poverty only a generation ago. But after two decades of unprecedented growth, the share in extreme poverty had more than halved. Globally, more than a billion people left the most destitute living conditions behind in just one generation. Since the 1980s, the share of the extreme poor has declined faster than ever before in world history, going down to below 10 percent of the global population by 2015. In absolute numbers extreme poverty decreased from nearly 1.9 billion people in 1990 to approximately 650 million in 2018. In fact, the rise of China and India alone was a game-changer. Their economic catching-up has led to a shift of the concentration of the poorest from Asia to Sub-Sahara Africa (Roser/Ortiz-Ospina 2019).

However, the remarkable MICs success story didn't happen all over the world. Most least-developed countries (LDCs)[39] remain trapped in cycles of entrenched poverty. They only have minuscule shares in world trade and global Foreign Direct Investment (FDI) flows, generate rather sluggish growth, and almost half of the population in the LDCs continues living in extreme poverty. None of these countries was able to meet the MDGs, and there are only scant chances that they will make considerable progress on the SDGs. In Sub-Sahara Africa, extreme poverty not only failed to be abated but even kept on rising from roughly 280 million people in 1990 to 418 million in 2015. Persistent cycles of poverty and deprivations often go hand in hand with deeply entrenched conflicts and crises (Stuart et al. 2016: 31–32).

In 2015, when the MDG era was coming to an end, the fight against poverty experienced, rather unexpectedly, an inflection point, and has been slowing down since then. Between 2015 and 2019, the global poverty rate fell by around 0.54 percentage points per year which is, disappointingly, less than half the average reduction between 2000 and 2014 (United Nations, Inter-agency Task Force on Financing for Development 2024: 30). The highest numbers of poor people are still living in MICs of which many are quite populous. However, the MICs have proven that they know how to tackle this challenge. While most of the upper-middle-income countries are rather confident about finishing the job, lower-middle-income countries are struggling a lot more to advance in the fight against poverty.

The much greater challenge, however, lies in enabling the LDCs to lift themselves out of their least-developed status. Even during the years 2000–2015, when the LDCs experienced robust economic growth at an average rate of seven percent, this was still not enough to enable them graduate from their LDC status. They remain the most susceptible to economic and environmental shocks. The combined crises of COVID-19 and its aftermath, climate change, and the most recent violent conflicts have pushed an additional 75–95 million people into extreme poverty. And the subsequent cost-of-living crisis with food and fuel prices at historic highs was responsible for an additional 78–141 million unable to escape poverty. Sadly, in 2024 the global poverty rate was higher than five years ago. About 8.5 percent of the global population lived in extreme poverty which is 692 million people living on less than $2.15 per person per day. Continued at the current pace, it would take decades to eliminate poverty. Projections are that extreme poverty will be staying over 7 percent until 2050. This means very clearly missing SDG 1 about ending extreme poverty by 2030 (United Nations 2023b: 7–10; World Bank 2024b: 58–59).

Since 2015, hunger is also on the rise. In 2019, about 7.9 percent of the global population were enduring chronic hunger, equivalent to 613 million people. In 2022, the respective numbers had jumped to 9.2 percent, or between 712 and 757 million people. After the pandemic, a quick recovery was missing, leading to about 733 million people suffering hunger in 2023. Similarly, the proportion of people experiencing food insecurity has risen from 22 percent in 2015 to 29 percent in 2023. This means also very clearly missing SDG 2 about zero hunger by 2030 (United Nations 2024: 8–10; World Bank 2024b: 201).

Geographically, Africa lags behind the most in achieving the SDGs. 26 of the 28 most vulnerable LDCs are in Sub-Sahara Africa, and they are projected to miss most of the human development targets. Sub-Sahara Africa is home to two-thirds of the global extreme poor. Crucial targets, such as reducing child mortality and underweight children, ensuring electricity or safe sanitation access are estimated to make only scant progress. Geographically, the fight against poverty will be decided in Sub-Sahara Africa (World Bank 2024b: 70–73).

One of the major causes for entrenched poverty and destitution are persistent violence and conflict. If these are not abated, chances are low that there will be decisive advances regarding stability, decent lives, and wellbeing. Obviously, in rather volatile and fragile places, financial flows are very unlikely to come in and improve the economic situation. Violence and conflict are almost certain to thwarting any kind of progress, and sadly, they are on the rise. In 2015, roughly 65 million people were forcibly displaced worldwide which was a shocking record at the time. In 2024, the number had risen to another shocking record with 120 million displaced people, almost double the number from 2015.[40] In 2023, roughly 2 billion people were living in conflict-affected areas which is almost one-quarter of humanity. The conflicts in Syria, Venezuela, Ukraine, Sudan/South Sudan, the Sahel, and Gaza are among the main drivers. Sub-Sahara Africa alone saw rising numbers of conflict-related casualties by 23 percent. Currently, the world is facing the highest number of violent conflicts since the Second World War. In 2021, global military expenditure, for the first time ever, exceeded $2 trillion (United Nations 2023b: 5–7, 2024: 29). Against this backdrop, it is hard to see how significant progress in the fight against poverty could be possible with conflicts, violence, and the number of affected people being on the rise. Unsurprisingly, war-torn and conflict-affected countries[41] rank the last on the 2024 SDG index scores.

While the rise of the MICs has impressively proven that it is possible to substantially reduce poverty at scale and within a short period of time, they concurrently experienced the downside of these glittering success stories. The "leaving behind poverty" party was turning into a heavy hangover with many MICs facing the harrowing flipside of breathtaking growth rates, rapid industrialization, and urbanization: skyrocketing air and water pollution, hazardous waste and toxic residues with all health issues included, as people were increasingly exposed to a degrading environment. These and other environmental issues were slingshot right into the heart of many MICs, and, frighteningly, they wouldn't just disappear with time. The long sought-after prosperity was coming with a bitter aftertaste and a deeply troubling price tag.

The developments of China and India contrast dramatically the boon and bane of catching-up on the speed lane with millions becoming middle-class consumers:

Some 30 years ago, China was where some of the poor countries are today – a backwater country whose economy made up hardly two percent of global GDP. But since then, China invested heavily in infrastructure and focused on propelling economic growth. Over decades, China's GDP has grown more than 10-fold. Between 2001 and 2011, Chinese GDP grew at an annual average rate of 10.5 percent, almost quadrupling the Chinese economy from $1.3 trillion to $4.98 trillion. Subsequently, China jumped from being the sixth-largest to the second-largest economy. In three decades, rapid economic growth lifted more than 800 million people out of extreme poverty. China's development alone had ripple effects around the world. Between 2000 and 2009, China's imports from the LDCs increased 24 percent annually.

By 2009, China had become the largest export destination of the LDCs, and one year later, it was the second-largest import destination for the European Union and the third largest for the USA (Newell et al. 2020: 23; Shepard 2019; World Bank 2024b: 64–65).

In India, a similar success story took place. With almost two-thirds of the population living in poverty in the 1970s, poverty rates have been declining since then consistently. Through large investments in health, water and sanitation, education, infrastructure, and other public programs targeting the areas with the lowest development indicators, millions of people were enabled to leave behind poverty. Particularly remarkable is how much poverty eradication accelerated. The rate of poverty reduction between 2012 and 2022 was roughly the same as during 30 years in the past. The beginning of 2024, India proudly announced the elimination of extreme poverty. Today, India is the fastest growing economy in the world, with GDP growth around 8 percent for two decades that lifted 300 million people out of extreme poverty. By 2028, India is set to become the third largest economy in the world, and is poised to reach a high-middle-income status by 2047 (Bhalla/Bhasin 2024; IEA 2024: 276–277).

But the downsides of these success stories were likewise enormous. From 1990 to 2015, primary energy demand tripled in China, and coal accounted for 69 percent of this growth. China turned into the world's largest CO_2 emitter with the subsequent air pollution impacts included. The World Bank already in 1995 pointed out that air pollution in China accounted for a GDP loss of 7.7 percent. But the low fines for polluters violating the law and the high costs for complying with the regulations, in fact, led to many dirty industries continuing to work and just pay the fines for many years. It took some tragic incidents before polluting and poisoning were not considered a minor negligence any more. In the 1990s, for example, the Huai River Basin was considered the most polluted river in China. Contaminated drinking water killed fish and birds, and caused epidemics and long-term diseases. Subsequently, in one of the single largest pollution abatement campaigns several thousand factories in the region were shut down (Bai/Shi 2006). There were alarming health impacts of notoriously bad air quality in big cities. Beijing even suffered an "airpocalypse" in 2013, that was eventually decisively ramping up government action. Between 2009 and 2012, China spent more than $35 billion to subsidize the electric-vehicle industry. Since then, many cities have experienced significant improvements in air quality. However, in other places high levels of air, water, and soil pollution continue being unabated (Maizland 2021; Malcomson 2020).

India is home to 63 of the 100 most polluted cities in the world with New Delhi as the capital with the worst air quality in the world.

It likewise took some severe incidents to ramp up government action. There are an estimated 7 million premature deaths each year because of air pollution. Eventually, in 2021, several large power plants around Delhi were shut down due to alarming levels of air quality. Starting in 2023, the use of coal as a fuel was banned in the National Capital Region. Water is equally polluted, and an estimated 70 percent of surface water is considered inadequate for human consumption with nearly 40 million Indians suffering from waterborne diseases (Igini 2024). However, while most Indians recognize climate change and its destructive effects, environmental issues are not making headlines as one would expect. While food, water, and health are considered much more important, the close link to climate change is still being overlooked and underestimated (*Times of India* 2024).

The unprecedented economic catching-up processes of many MICs showcased dramatically the double-edged sword of driving on the fast lane of development. Acknowledging how much fighting poverty and protecting the environment were intertwined and could not be tackled separately, eventually led to the merging of the poverty and the environmental agenda as decided in Rio in 2012. The post-2015 process accelerated debunking the myth about growing first and cleaning up later being a success formula. Much to the contrary, this turned out to be a fatally flawed thinking, and the idea of "pollute now and develop and deal with it later" was increasingly dismissed. Ecological degradation was not a luxury concern that poor countries could postpone dealing with until they thought they could afford it. Instead, it had become evident that all countries, no matter the development stage, had to transition toward economies that are respecting the limits of nature on which human wellbeing unequivocally depends on (Bai/Shi 2006; Malcomson 2020; Raworth 2017: 206–211).

When millions of people are enabled to get out of poverty and eventually lead a middle-class life, this inevitably causes dramatic changes at scale in consumption of goods and services, housing, energy, mobility, etc. And the global middle class keeps on expanding. It was only around 1985 that 1 billion people had reached some middle-class status. It then took 21 years until 2006, to add another billion, much of this stemming from China's extraordinary growth. And after that, it took only nine years to globally have an additional third billion of people as middle-class consumers (Kharas 2017: 11).

In addition to the expanding middle class, demography keeps on further mounting the pressure. The sheer numbers speak for themselves. In 1960, the world was inhabited by 3 billion people, in 1999 it was 6 billion people, and in 2019 the number had risen to 7.7 billion. Although population growth peaked in the 1970s and 1980s and is slowing down since the 2000s, it is estimated that by 2038 the world might have to sustain 9 billion people, and by 2056 this number might be at 10 billion. This increase will take place mostly in the less developed and emerging regions in Asia and Africa. By 2050, Africa's 1.1 billion people population is slated to double and reach more than 4 billion by 2100, with 80 percent of this growth happening in cities (Ritchie 2019; Shepard 2019).

For the world's ecosystems and resources, the repercussions could be disastrous. To meet the future food demand of 9–10 billion people, the current agricultural output would have to increase by an additional 70 percent. However, producing more food for the remaining poor to escape poverty and to satisfy the demand of a growing population will only be sustainable, and thus in line with the SDGs, if this happens without raising high-intensive agriculture, global energy and water consumption, or even better lowering it and, of course, also lowering greenhouse gas emissions (Ceres2030 2020: 8–9; Morgan Stanley 2020: 12; UNDESA 2014: 21–26). Very unsurprisingly, this looks like an impossible mission.

Regarding water, the prospects are equally deeply troubling. At current population growth and development pace, by 2030 two billion people will remain without access to save drinking water. The gap between global demand and supplies of fresh water is expected to reach 40 percent. Water use has been increasing worldwide by about one percent per year since the 1980s with agriculture being by far the largest water consumer. Agriculture accounts for about 70 percent of global freshwater withdrawals and is set to increase by more than 50 percent by 2050 with a view to feeding a growing global population (Morgan Stanley 2022; United Nations 2024: 20–21).

Regarding energy, the potential developments are equally worrying. Several projections assume that world energy consumption will grow by between 30 to almost 50 percent until 2050, depending on the impact and ambition of climate-related policies and measures. Improvements in energy efficiency and behavioral change are likely to be outpaced by a growing population, rising incomes and a subsequent shift to more energy-intensive goods and services. Energy demand is set to increase more than two and a half times until 2050, if the economic and demographic dynamics persist. The industrial sector is expected to grow by far the strongest with up to 60 percent. The fastest growth will be happening in India where by 2050 industrial energy consumption is assumed to double or maybe even triple. The same applies to Asia and Africa in general, where consumption is also expected to skyrocket (EIA 2023: 8–15; IEA 2021a: 14–18, 2021b; Newell et al. 2020: 8).

The seemingly intractable challenge in dire need of sustainable solutions at scale is to feed more people with less water, land, and energy.

The urgency to act is dramatically underscored by the already alarming state of many ecosystems and the continuing degradation of nature. The loss of ocean biodiversity due to human activities, including exploitation, industrial waste and agricultural runoff polluting rivers and oceans, continues unabated. Ocean acidification, overfishing, and mounting plastic pollution leaves SDG 14 (protecting the oceans) largely out of reach. The same applies to the daunting prospects of achieving SDG 15 (protecting terrestrial ecosystems). The loss of biodiversity and forests, land degradation and desertification, continues unabated. An expanding agriculture is the main driver for most of the ongoing deforestation and habitat loss, resulting in a further degradation of soils and extinction of species (United Nations 2024: 36–39).

It has been aptly written about climate change and it impacts on the earth's ecosystems and human life. The climate pledge of reducing global emissions by at least 50 percent by 2030 and reaching net-zero CO_2 emissions by 2050, is largely out of reach. Since the adoption of the Paris Agreement and the SDGs in 2015, the progress in reducing greenhouse gas emissions is still too little and too slow to reduce emissions fast enough to prevent the adverse impacts of climate change. Projections see a wide range of scenarios, between cutting emissions by 16 percent or increasing them by more than 30 percent by 2050, very much depending on growth rates, costs of fossil fuels, and energy and climate policies (EIA 2023: 38–40). Adaptation across the world is only fragmented and unequal, and dedicated resources and engagement, so far, are too limited to turn the tide. Current policies set the world on track for warming by 2–3 degrees Celsius. The chances of limiting warming to 1.5 degrees lie by only 14 percent (IPCC 2023; United Nations 2024: 34; World Bank 2024b: 23).

It doesn't take much wisdom to see the disaster looming at the horizon, leading to future doomsday scenarios: If the global population reaches between 9 and 10 billion people by 2050, and if the rate of poor people turning into middle-class consumers continues at the same speed and scale, several planet earths will be needed to sustain current lifestyles with the current material footprint and the current human impact on nature. If everyone lived like current Americans, more than five earths would be needed to only satisfy material needs.[42] It is very unlikely that humanity would survive such a global overshoot beyond planetary boundaries and an unabated polluting and degrading of the earth's ecosystems (Raworth 2017: 210–211). The 2030 Agenda remains silent on the topic of demography as it ushered in too much vitriol during the post-2015 negotiations. But science is clear about the sustainability challenges that relentlessly keep on sounding the alarm bells: population growth combined with rising food and energy demand, rising resource use and consumption as well as climate change and degrading ecosystems are a fatal combination. Enabling all humankind to lead a decent life has the potential to usher in either option: a blissful new era on earth, fulfilling the noble objective to eventually free all people from fear and want and living according to nature's cycles and capacities, or an environmental disaster, damaging the natural ecosystems beyond repair and leaving some parts of the earth uninhabitable for humans. Hence, going sustainable is not simply an option, it is imperative for the survival of humankind. And the SDGs, despite all flaws and shortcomings, are pointing the way and mark the challenges that need to be addressed unequivocally for a better world.

Notes

1 https://databank.worldbank.org/source/worldwide-governance-indicators
2 https://rsf.org/en/index
3 https://academic-freedom-index.net/
4 https://www.transparency.org/en/cpi/2023
5 https://www.v-dem.net/
6 https://freedomhouse.org/countries/freedom-world/scores
7 https://www.worldbank.org/en/news/factsheet/2022/05/02/fact-sheet-an-adjustment-to-global-poverty-lines
8 https://www.unodc.org/documents/data-and-analysis/statistics/corruption/UNODC_Statistical_Framework_to_measure_corruption.pdf
9 https://fsc.org/en
10 https://www.msc.org/
11 https://www.fairtrade.net/
12 https://www.usgbc.org/leed
13 https://neweconomics.org/2006/07/happy-planet-index
14 https://epi.yale.edu/
15 https://www.worldwildlife.org/industries/palm-oil
16 https://rspo.org/
17 https://www.who.int/news-room/fact-sheets/detail/ambient-(outdoor)-air-quality-and-health
18 https://www.sdgsynergies.org/
19 https://knowsdgs.jrc.ec.europa.eu/enablingsdgs
20 https://www.millennium-institute.org/sustainable-development-simulator
21 https://ambitiontoaction.net/scan_tool/
22 https://www.iea.org/data-and-statistics/data-product/fossil-fuel-subsidies-database
23 https://www.footprintnetwork.org/
24 https://www.thecaq.org/sp-500-and-esg-reporting
25 https://www.globalreporting.org/
26 https://www.ifrs.org/groups/international-sustainability-standards-board/
27 Directive (EU) 2022/2464
28 https://climatechampions.unfccc.int/
29 https://www.unepfi.org/net-zero-alliance/
30 https://www.breakthroughenergy.org/
31 https://initiatives.weforum.org/first-movers-coalition/home
32 https://pledge.zerohungercoalition.org/en
33 https://www.worldbenchmarkingalliance.org/
34 https://www.unpri.org/

35 https://www.icmagroup.org/sustainable-finance/the-principles-guidelines-and-handbooks/green-bond-principles-gbp/
36 https://gisdalliance.org/
37 https://focus2030.org/Special-Edition-New-global-financing-pact-what-to-expect-from-the-June-22-23
38 https://www.worldbank.org/en/country/mic/overview
39 In 2024, 44 countries were designated by the United Nations as "least developed countries" (LDCs), based on the criteria per-capita income, human asset (nutrition, health, school enrolment, literacy), and economic vulnerability. These were: Afghanistan, Angola, Bangladesh, Benin, Burkina Faso, Burundi, Cambodia, Central African Republic, Chad, Comoros, Democratic Republic of the Congo, Djibouti, Eritrea, Ethiopia, Gambia, Guinea, Guinea-Bissau, Haiti, Kiribati, Lao People's Democratic Republic, Lesotho, Liberia, Madagascar, Malawi, Mali, Mauritania, Mozambique, Myanmar, Nepal, Niger, Rwanda, Senegal, Sierra Leone, Solomon Islands, Somalia, South Sudan, Sudan, Timor-Leste, Togo, Tuvalu, Uganda, Tanzania, Yemen, and Zambia.
40 https://www.migrationdataportal.org/
41 Niger, Congo, Afghanistan, Yemen, Somalia, Chad, Central African Republic, South Sudan
42 https://overshoot.footprintnetwork.org/how-many-earths-or-countries-do-we-need/

References

Alonso, José Antonio (2012): From Aid to Global Development Policy, UNDESA Working Paper No. 121, ST/ESA/2012/DWP/121, September 2012.

Atasu, Atalay/Serasu Duran/Luk N. Wassenhove (2021): The Dark Side of Solar Power. *Harvard Business Review*, June 18, 2021.

Bai, Xuemei/Peijun Shi (2006): Pollution Control in China's Huai River Basin: What Lessons for Sustainability? *ResearchGate Environment*, Vol. 48, No. 7, September 2006. https://dx.doi.org/10.3200/ENVT.48.7.22-38

Bennich, Therese/Åsa Persson/Raphaëlle Beaussart/Cameron Allen/Shirin Malekpour (2023): Recurring Patterns of SDG Linkages and How They Can Advance the 2030 Agenda. *One Earth*, Vol. 6, November 17, 2023. https://doi.org/10.1016/j.oneear.2023.10.008

Bhalla, Surjit S./Karan Bashin (2024): India Eliminates Extreme Poverty. *Brookings*, March 1, 2024. https://www.brookings.edu/articles/india-eliminates-extreme-poverty/

BlackRock (2019): *An Evolution in ESG Indexing*. iShares by BlackRock Inc.

Bonnedahl, Karl Johan/Pasi Heikkurinen/Jouni Paavola (2022): Strongly Sustainable Development Goals: Overcoming Distances Constraining Responsible Action. *Environmental Science and Policy*, Vol. 129, pp. 150–158.

Bothello, Joel et al. (2023): How Some Companies Avoid Accusations of Greenwashing, *Harvard Business Review*, September 27, 2023.

Ceres2030 (2020): *Sustainable Solutions to End Hunger*, Cornell University, IFPRI and IISD. https://www.ifpri.org/project/ceres2030-sustainable-solutions-end-hunger/

Deloitte (2023): The Sustainable Consumer 2023. https://www.deloitte.com/uk/en/Industries/consumer/research/sustainable-consumer.html

EIA – U.S. Energy Information Administration (2023): International Energy Outlook 2023, October 2023, Washington DC.

Eisenmenger, Nina/Melanie Pichler/Nora Krenmayr/Dominik Noll/Barbara Plank/Ekaterina Schalmann/Marie-Theres Wandl/Simone Gingrich (2020): The Sustainable Development Goals Prioritize Economic Growth over Sustainable Resource Use: A Critical Reflection on the SDGs from a Socio-ecological Perspective. *Sustainability Science*, Vol. 15, pp. 1101–1110.

Galiana, Isabel (2018): Benefits and Costs of the Energy Targets for the Post-2015 Development Agenda, in: Bjorn Lomborg (Ed.): *Prioritizing Development. A Cost Benefit Analysis of the United Nations' Sustainable Development Goals*, Copenhagen Consensus Center, pp. 143–167. Cambridge University Press.

Herrington, Gaya (2021): Update to Limits to Growth: Comparing the World3 Model with Empirical Data. *Journal of Industrial Ecology*, Vol. 25, pp. 614–626. https://doi.org/10.1111/jiec.13084

Hestad, Dina (2021): The Evolution of Private Sector Action in Sustainable Development, in: International Institute for Sustainable Development (ISSD), Earth Negotiations Bulletin Brief #12.

Hickel, Jason (2018): Why Growth Can't Be Green. *Foreign Policy*, September 12, 2018.

Hickel, Jason (2019): The Contradiction of the Sustainable Development Goals: Growth versus Ecology on a Finite Planet. *Sustainable Development*. https://doi.org/10.1002/sd.1947

Holger, Dieter (2022): The Solar Boom Will Create Millions of Tons of Junk Panels. *Wall Street Journal, Sustainable Business*, 5 May 2022.

Howe, Ben Ryder (2023): New Skyscraper, Built to Be an Environmental Marvel, Is Already Dated. *New York Times*, February 14, 2023.

IEA – International Energy Agency (2021a): Net Zero by 2050. A Roadmap for the Global Energy Sector, May 2021, Paris.

IEA – International Energy Agency (2021b): World Energy Outlook 2021, Paris. https://www.iea.org/reports/world-energy-outlook-2021

IEA – International Energy Agency (2024): World Energy Outlook 2024, Paris. https://www.iea.org/reports/world-energy-outlook-2024

IEA/IRENA/UNSD/World Bank/ WHO (2024): Tracking SDG 7: The Energy Progress Report, World Bank, Washington DC.

Igini, Martina (2024): 5 Biggest Environmental Issues in India. *Earth.org*, May 30th, 2024, https://earth.org/environmental-issues-in-india/

IPCC – The Intergovernmental Panel on Climate Change (2019): Climate Change and Land: An IPCC Special Report on Climate Change, Desertification, Land Degradation, Sustainable Land Management, Food Security, and Greenhouse Gas Fluxes in Terrestrial Ecosystems, Geneva.

IPCC – The Intergovernmental Panel on Climate Change (2023): Climate Change 2023: Synthesis Report, Geneva.

IRENA – International Renewable Energy Agency (2016): End-of-Life Management Solar Photovoltaic Panels, Abu Dhabi, June 2016.

IRENA – International Renewable Energy Agency (2024): Renewable Power Generation Cost in 2023, Abu Dhabi.

Jackson, Tim (2017): *Prosperity without Growth, Foundations for the Economy of Tomorrow*, Second Edition, London/New York: Routledge.

Jerven, Morten (2018): The Cost and Benefit of Data Needed to Monitor the Post-2015 Development Agenda, in: Bjorn Lomborg (Ed.): *Prioritizing*

Development. A Cost Benefit Analysis of the United Nations' Sustainable Development Goals, Copenhagen Consensus Center, pp. 91–116. Cambridge University Press.

Kapto, Serge (2019): Layers of Politics and Power Struggles in the SDG Indicators Process. *Global Policy*, Vol. 10, Suppl. 1, pp. 134–136.

Kaufmann, Daniel (2021): It's Complicated: Lessons from 25 Years of Measuring Governance. *Brookings Institution, Blog Future Development.* https://www.brookings.edu/blog/future-development/2021/09/30/its-complicated-lessons-from-25-years-of-measuring-governance/

Kharas, Homi (2017): The Unprecedented Expansion of the Global Middle Class, Global Economy & Development, Working Paper 100, February 2017.

Kharas, Homi/Charlotte Rivard (2023): Financing the Sustainable Development Goals: The Big Stuck, in: Dag Hammarskjöld Foundation (Ed.): *Financing the UN Development System: Choices in Uncertain Times*, September 2023, pp. 112–119. Uppsala, Sweden: Dag Hammarskjöld Foundation.

Kubiszewski, Ida/Kenneth Mulder/Diane Jarvis/Robert Costanza (2021): Toward Better Measurement of Sustainable Development and Wellbeing: A Small Number of SDG Indicators Reliably Predict Life Satisfaction. *Sustainable Development*, Vol. 30, pp. 139–148, https://onlinelibrary.wiley.com/doi/epdf/10.1002/sd.2234

Laborde, David/Sophia Murphy/Marie Parent/Jaron Porciello/Carin Smaller (2020): *Ceres2030: Sustainable Solutions to End Hunger – Summary Report*, Cornell University, IFPRI and IISD. https://www.ifpri.org/project/ceres2030-sustainable-solutions-end-hunger/

Lopes, Flavia (2024): Clean Energy's Dirty Secret: The Trail of Waste Left by India's Solar Power Boom. *The Guardian*, April 18, 2024.

MacFeely, Steve (2020): Measuring the Sustainable Development Goal Indicators: An Unprecedented Statistical Challenge. *Journal of Official Statistics*, Vol. 36, No. 2, pp. 361–378.

Maizland, Lindsay (2021): China's Fight Against Climate Change and Environmental Degradation, *Council on Foreign Relations*, May 19, 2021.

Malcomson, Scott (2020): How China Became the World's Leader in Green Energy. *Foreign Affairs*, February 28, 2020.

Manuel, Marcus/Harsh Desai/Emma Samman/Martin Evans (2018): *Financing the End of Extreme Poverty*, London: Overseas Development Institute, September 2018.

Martin, Matthew/Jo Walker (2015): Financing the Sustainable Development Goals. Lessons from government spending on the MDGs, Government Spending Watch Report, Development Finance International/Oxfam.

McNeill, John Robert/Peter Engelke (2014): *The Great Acceleration, an Environmental History of the Anthropocene since 1945*, Cambridge, MA: Harvard University.

Morgan Stanley (2020): The Future of Food: Complexities and Compromises. *Blue Paper*, December 6, 2020.

Morgan Stanley (2022): A Deep Dive on the Water Crisis, February 14, 2022. https://www.morganstanley.com/ideas/water-scarcity-causes-and-solutions

Nelson, Jane (2018): Collective Action on Business Standards, Goals, and Metrics to Achieve Scale and Impact for the SDGs, in: Raj M. Desai/Hiroshi Kato/Homi Kharas/John W. McArthur (Eds.): *From Summits to Solutions.*

Innovations in Implementing the Sustainable Development Goals, Washington D.C.: The Brookings Institution, pp. 80–105.
Newell, Richard G./Daniel Raimi/Seth Villanueva/Brian Pest (2020): Global Energy Outlook 2020: Energy Transition or Energy Addition? Resources for the Future, Report 20-05, May 2020, Washington DC.
Parker, Laura (2024): The World's Plastic Pollution Crisis, Explained. *National Geographic,* September 23, 2024.
Plumer, Brad/Nadja Popovich (2019): These Countries Have Prices on Carbon. Does It Work? *New York Times*, April 2, 2019.
Pradhan, Prajal/Luis Costa/Diego Rybski/Wolfgang Lucht/Jürgen P. Kropp (2017): A Systematic Study of Sustainable Development Goal (SDG) Interactions. *Earth's Future*, Vol. 5, pp. 1169–1179.
Raworth, Kate (2017): *Doughnut Economics. Seven Ways to Think Like a 21st-Century Economist*, Random House Business, London.
Reichheld, Ashley/John Peto/Cory Ritthaler (2023): Research: Consumers' Sustainability Demands Are Rising. *Harvard Business Review, Business and Society*, September 18, 2023.
Ritchie, Hannah (2019): More Than 8 Out of 10 People in the World Will Live in Asia or Africa by 2100. Retrieved from: https://ourworldindata.org/region-population-2100 [Online Resource]
Ritchie, Hannah/Max Roser (2021): Forests and Deforestation. Published online at OurWorldInData.org. Retrieved from: https://ourworldindata.org/forests-and-deforestation [Online Resource]
Ritchie, Hannah/Veronika Samborska/Max Roser (2023): Plastic Pollution. Published online at OurWorldInData.org. Retrieved from: https://ourworldindata.org/plastic-pollution [Online Resource]
Roser, Max/Esteban Ortiz-Ospina (2019): Global Extreme Poverty. Published online at OurWorldInData.org. Retrieved from: https://ourworldindata.org/extreme-poverty [Online Resource]
Sachs, Jeffrey/Guillaume Lafortune/Grayson Fuller (2024): The SDGs and the UN Summit of the Future. Sustainable Development Report 2024, New York, London, Paris. https://files.unsdsn.org/sustainable-development-report-2024.pdf
Sanwal, Mukul (2015): *The World's Search for Sustainable Development, a Perspective from the Global South*, Cambridge: Cambridge University Press.
Shepard, Wade (2019): What China Is Really Up to in Africa, *Forbes,* October 3, 2019.
Songwe, Vera (2023): Carbon pricing: an integral part of a just transition, in: Dag Hammarskjöld Foundation (Ed.): *Financing the UN Development System: Choices in Uncertain Times*, September 2023, pp. 123-125.
Stuart, Elizabeth et al. (2016): Leaving No One Behind, a Critical Path for the First 1,000 Days of the Sustainable Development Goals, ODI (Overseas Development Institute), London.
Svizzero, Serge/Clement Allan Tisdell (2015): The Post-2015 Global Development Agenda: A Critical Analysis, July 4, 2015, Researchgate. https://www.researchgate.net/publication/279573032
The White House, Office of Information and Regulatory Affairs (2023): Guidance for Assessing Changes in Environmental and Ecosystem Services in Benefit-Cost-Analysis, Washington DC.

Times of India (2024): Political Disconnect: Why Environmental Issues Are Not Winning Votes in India. *Times of India*, March 17, 2024.

UN High-Level Expert Group on the Net Zero Emissions Commitments of Non-State Entities (2022): Integrity Matters: Net Zero Commitments by Businesses, Financial Institutions, Cities and Regions, November 2022.

UNCTAD (2021): World Investment Report, Geneva.

UNDESA (2014): TST Issues Briefs, a Compendium of Issues Briefs Prepared by the United Nations Inter-Agency Technical Support Team for the United Nations General Assembly Open Working Group on Sustainable Development Goals, New York.

UNDP (2016): From the MDGs to Sustainable Development for all, Lessons from 10 Years of Practice, New York.

UNEP (2024a): Global Waste Management Outlook: Beyond an Age of Waste – Turning Rubbish into a Resource, Nairobi.

UNEP (2024b): Critical Transitions: Circularity, Equity and Responsibility in the Quest for Energy Transition Minerals, Working Paper, Nairobi. https://www.unep.org/resources/publication/critical-transitions-circularity-equity-and-responsibility-quest-energy

United Nations (2015): The Millennium Development Goals Report 2015, New York.

United Nations (2021): The Sustainable Development Goals Report 2021, New York.

United Nations (2023a): The Sustainable Development Goals Report 2023, New York.

United Nations (2023b): Global Sustainable Development Report 2023: Times of Crisis, Times of Change: Science for Accelerating Transformations for Sustainable Development, New York.

United Nations (2024): The Sustainable Development Goals Report 2024, New York.

United Nations et al. (2021): System of Environmental-Economic Accounting—Ecosystem Accounting (SEEA EA). White Cover Publication. https://seea.un.org/ecosystem-accounting

United Nations, Inter-agency Task Force on Financing for Development (2020): Financing for Sustainable Development Report 2020, New York.

United Nations, Inter-agency Task Force on Financing for Development (2024): Financing for Sustainable Development Report 2024: Financing for Development at a Crossroads, New York.

van Vuuren, Detlef P./Caroline Zimm/Sebastian Busch/Armin von Schiller/Jörn O. Schmidt/Bjoern Soergel (2022): Defining a sustainable development target space for 2030 and 2050. *One Earth*, Vol. 5, No. 2, pp. 142–156.Vol. 21, No. 3, pp. 40–47. https://doi.org/10.48558/0DPW-ZM76

Williams, Amanda/Patrick Haack/Knut Haanaes (2023): Putting the SDGs Back on Track, *Stanford Social Innovation Review*, 21(3), 40–47. https://doi.org/10.48558/0DPW-ZM76

World Bank (2024a): Sustainable Development Bonds & Green Bonds: Impact Report 2023, Washington DC.

World Bank (2024b): Poverty, Prosperity, and Planet Report 2024: Pathways Out of the Polycrisis, Washington DC.

5

LEARNING FROM AND LOOKING BEYOND THE SDGs

Going sustainable is here to stay as a question of survival for humankind

On the road to 2030: No one said it would be easy

Since 2015, every year the SDG crowd meets in New York at the United Nations (UN) to discuss and analyze the state of play of the SDGs and to exchange about how to tackle setbacks and accelerate progress. During the post-2015 negotiations, governments were full of skepticism and wariness toward a compulsory monitoring and follow-up mechanism. They were afraid of being literally summoned to the UN and painfully grilled about progress on the SDGs or lack of thereof. Thus, an independent in-depth review, pinpointing to deficits and issuing recommendations, from the start, never had a chance. But very unexpectedly, both the yearly High-level Political Forum (HLPF) and the SDG summits every four years have turned into highly appreciated occasions for debating the SDGs and a more sustainable world. Over the years, governments have developed an astonishing enthusiasm and willingness to be part of the review game in which they increasingly engage (Donoghue 2020). By 2021, around two-thirds of governments globally had developed some kind of SDG strategy or had incorporated the SDGs into their national planning. Every year, between 40 and 50 member states submit a Voluntary National Review (VNR) and engage in a subsequent debate with peers, some already for the second or third time[1] (United Nations 2023b: 30–31).

However, due to the voluntary nature of the follow-up and the self-reporting of the VNRs, governments usually prefer praising their respective efforts and dodging and concealing controversies or setbacks. Critical goals, such as inequality, consumption and production, or the environmental goals are often neglected, and the quality of many VNRs in general is rather mediocre. Most VNRs "are largely descriptive and lack analytical depth and policy focus, do not reflect efforts that match the ambition of the agenda or its integrated concept…" (Fukuda-Parr

DOI: 10.4324/9781032702681-5

et al. 2023: 5). To make them valuable and insightful reports and a real tool for mutual learning, the reporting countries would have to be much more self-critical, open, and self-reflecting regarding specific country challenges and lessons learned, what is accelerating progress and what is slowing it down. Also, many VNRs dodge thorny issues, such as exclusion, discrimination, or migration and displacement (Fukuda-Parr et al. 2023: 4–6). But, no one seriously expected a catharsis-like openness or relentless self-criticism. Interestingly, some countries adapt the SDGs to make them fit into their national agendas, bolstering the legitimacy of their policies through cherry-picking and reinterpreting the goals they deem relevant (Beisheim 2023: 12–13). As there are no common reporting standards, which member states had refused defining during the post-2015 negotiations, the VNRs are also difficult to compare. UNDESA published a compilation of best practices to showcase what good reporting can look like (UNDESA 2022).

An interesting complementary tool are the civil society reports, the so-called shadow reports. These reports supplement or present a different perspective on the SDGs in their respective countries and, thus, ensure that monitoring and stocktaking at the HLPF is not a government show, only. Even cities and regions have jumped on the SDG bandwagon and are increasingly engaged in voluntarily reporting on their progress toward the SDGs. In 2017, subnational entities in Brazil, Spain, Australia, Belgium, and the Philippines were the first to deliver such a report. With the beginning of 2024, around 200 "Voluntary Local Reviews" were available (Biermann et al. 2022).

While UN member countries are praising their respective efforts and achievements in the VNRs, the sound of the alarm bells from the UN and many other sources about very much failing the promise of the 2030 Agenda are turning louder and more urgent. Over the years, the regular official reports have become increasingly alarming. In 2019, the UN Secretary-General denoted that "the transformation required to meet the Sustainable Development Goals by 2030 is not yet advancing at the speed or scale required" (United Nations 2019: 2). A couple of years later, he was much more dramatic in his warnings about the SDGs "disappearing in the rear-view mirror" (United Nations 2023a: 4), and even about the need to "rescue the SDGs" (United Nations 2024: 2). In 2023, the group of independent scientists, tasked with publishing the Global Sustainable Development Report every four years, equally issued a forceful warning: "Without course correction and acceleration, humanity will face prolonged periods of crisis and uncertainty – triggered by and reinforcing poverty, inequality, hunger, disease, conflict and disaster" (United Nations 2023b: XVIII).

At their midpoint, only 17 percent of the SDGs were on track, while one-third of the targets have seen no progress, or even worse, regression below the 2015 baseline. Roughly half of the SDGs were moderately or severely off track (United Nations 2024: 4). In fact, in none of the three dimensions of sustainable development, social, economic, and environmental, is progress satisfactory, let alone a true transformation happening. Significantly advancing on the unfinished business of the MDGs and eradicating poverty, at least extreme poverty, would be an essential accomplishment, in particular given that the original promise dates back from 2000. But despite some positive trends, poverty and hunger are on the rise. Significantly lowering greenhouse gas emissions and the human material footprint, reducing waste, pollution, and depletion would be an important sign for making clear progress toward a sustainable economy. But this is neither the case. And finally, clear advances in protecting and restoring ecosystems, biodiversity and the natural world in general would be crucial for improving the state of the earth. But the environmental dimension, very worryingly, lags behind the most. When looking at the two overarching aims of the 2030 Agenda, eradicating poverty and transforming all human activities on earth to make them respect planetary boundaries, they are not even close.

Considering the long-term global experience in fighting poverty and the tremendous successes during the MDG era, one would have expected the greatest progress on the so-called left-overs from the MDGs, the unfinished business of eradicating poverty. But very disappointingly, this is not the case. The aftermath of the pandemic has even led to the first rise in extreme poverty in a generation and effectively erased three years of progress in poverty alleviation. Very sadly, the World Bank already called the years 2020–2030 a “lost decade” in the fight against poverty (United Nations 2021: 26; World Bank 2024b: 50).

There are various reasons for this slowing down in eradicating poverty: a more complex and work-intensive global agenda since 2015, with resources going to social, economic, and environmental challenges alike, and deeply entrenched pockets of poverty due to conflict, violence, and recurring crises that are feeding and reinforcing each other. And with record numbers of displaced people and almost a quarter of humanity living in conflict-affected areas, it is hard to see how significant advances in the fight against poverty should be achieved. As long as derailing crises and devastating wars continue, it will be impossible to eliminate poverty in these countries, let alone reach the other SDGs.

Frustratingly, as discussed, poverty eradication doesn’t follow easy to replicate success models, applicable throughout the world. Instead, this is a most complex task, very much depending on the specific situation.

Pandemic-related setbacks and worsening geopolitical divides and wars, have nothing but hampered and stymied development efforts, broadly suffocating progress, in particular for the most vulnerable. However, it is also true that the SDGs were already off track before this confluence of crises was happening, and the pace of poverty eradication was clearly too slow before 2020 (United Nations 2019; World Bank 2024b: 58–59). Therefore, blaming the little progress and setbacks exclusively on these events doesn't reflect the full picture. But undoubtedly, the poorest and most vulnerable countries have obviously been hit the hardest by the simultaneous crises, including mounting effects of climate change, and have been the least able to adapt or recover. This shows the gap between the global SDG index score and that of poor countries which was larger in 2023 than in 2015 (Sachs et al. 2024: 15–16).

Regarding transforming all human activities to make them respect planetary boundaries, the other overarching aim of the 2030 Agenda, the situation is equally dismal. The envisaged economic transformation is only very slowly taking up speed, and the environmental goals are far off track. Rising temperatures, unabated pollution and greenhouse gas emissions, a skyrocketing material footprint and increasing mountains of waste and residues, ongoing biodiversity loss and deforestation are testimony to the miserable state of play of nature and the continued overstretching of planetary boundaries.

Some of the major impediments thwarting more progress have been discussed. The sustainability journey requires long-term decision-making for dismantling and resetting established economic and social patterns. And the required changes are of a fundamental nature, affecting entire economies as well as daily habits and treasured comforts. This is hampered by several factors: the short time horizon of electoral cycles and shareholder-value principles give priority to present needs and demands, relegating long-term impacts to the back seat. Also, governments or corporate boards are accountable to a limited number of people that are not necessarily affected by harmful decisions from a sustainability point of view. There is a considerable disconnect between those taking decisions and those potentially bearing the brunt of the burden. They might live on another continent or they might live in the future. In any case, because of this social, temporal, and geographic disconnect, the wrongdoers will rather unlikely be confronted with those suffering, and those initiating transformative change are unlikely to reap the benefits from bold decisions and policies. This makes it even more difficult to pursue and implement consistent and uncompromising policies over many years from a sustainability point of view. Current political stability, financial crises, or political and economic competition always appear more urgent and more imperative (Bonnedahl et al. 2022: 153).

The same applies to people and their daily decisions. Many people see and believe that the energy and the goods and services they consume every day affect the environment and the climate, but they do not believe in their ability to change that. The huge time gap between consumption decisions and their environmental impact leads to an unhealthy disconnect between cause and effect of pollution, depletion, and a deteriorating environment. Beyond a general knowledge about environmentally harmful factors and impacts, it is often extremely difficult to nail it down who or what was the culprit for specific environmental developments or incidents.

Of course, not all is doom and gloom, but obviously things go awry, and with more than half of the implementation time elapsed, there is no way denying that this is not the comprehensive transformation at the speed and scale envisaged in 2015. There are important successes, such as crucial advances in fighting HIV/AIDS or reducing child mortality. However, overall progress is far too slow for the 2030 deadline and, most importantly, too slow to prevent crossing planetary boundaries and hitting catastrophic tipping points (Kharas/McArthur 2024).

Furthermore, in several countries nationalist and populist governments that are rather hurting the cause of a global sustainability agenda came into power. They made it popular to explicitly not follow whatever was emanating from the multilateral UN system, in particular if it was supposedly hurting national economic interests. The global impact is even more dramatic the bigger those countries with nationalist governments are and the bigger the steps these take are. The US, for example, withdrew from the Paris Climate Agreement under the Trump administration in 2020 denouncing it as supposedly burdening American workers and businesses in an unfair way, but rejoined under the Biden administration in 2021. In 2025, the US again announced its withdrawal from the Paris Agreement and even officially rejected the SDGs and the global framework. Brazil under the administration of President Bolsonaro disengaged from the sustainable development agenda in 2019 and abandoned most international cooperation on environmental protection after his predecessors had been rather active in sustainability policies.

When looking at the SDGs themselves, which features propel or hinder their achievement, there are many revealing insights and lessons learned. Some shortcomings were already baked into the SDGs, resulting from their political creation process and the difficult endeavor of merging the poverty and the environmental agenda. Other weaknesses became apparent only later with their implementation: they are not binding, they are vastly underfunded, they are too vague and too numerous, and they are not immune from politics. The latter point has already been discussed, that the needed long-term decisions and long-term commitments are often undermined by short-term horizons such as the next elections or the next quarterly financial reports for stock analysts and investors. The point about the SDGs not being binding, indeed, largely makes the follow-up a good will exercise. However, legally binding SDGs would have never been possible to adopt at the UN. The negotiations already were an arduous and difficult journey that would have never resulted in such a comprehensive agenda, if the aspiration had been to make the SDGs legally binding. Drafting this rather ambitious agenda was, in fact, precisely possible because there are no penalizing measures. Creating group and public pressure during the regular follow-up to push for the SDG cause was the maximum member states were willing to agree to.

The point about the SDGs being underfunded is, indeed, one of the key linchpins eventually deciding if, where and how change will be happening. Financing questions have been haunting summits and international agendas for decades. The World Bank/IMF input "From Billions to Trillions" from 2015 appeared exaggerated and lurid at the time when the SDG crowd gathered in Addis to decide about the financing for the SDGs. But as it turned out, it couldn't have been closer to the truth. Igniting a once-in-a-generation deep and thorough transformation of this magnitude will only happen with the billions and trillions of dollars making this possible. But as illustrated, funding is far too little, and public but most of all private investment is woefully lacking to turn the tide. Despite some trailblazing and inspiring initiatives about investing for sustainable development, much more funding needs to be mobilized and catalyzed to ignite a true global transformation. However, when talking about financing gaps, it is essential to concurrently talk about how additional funding should be spent, as more money doesn't necessarily achieve more and better results.

The further criticism about the SDGs being too numerous and too vague is another valid point. As discussed, there are significant quality differences between the goals and targets, some targets are very specific and quantified, focusing on crucial and game-changing issues, and others are very generic recommendations and encouragements. Accordingly, missing the target on primary and secondary education for all girls and boys or the target on environmentally sound management of chemicals undoubtedly bears more severe consequences than missing the target on access to green and public spaces or the target on promoting sustainable tourism. In particular on economic and environmental issues, many targets are too soft, too unspecific, and too little pushing for going beyond traditional growth, or clearly delineating natural boundaries as the red lines (Hestad 2021: 5–6).

Considering the dire situation of the natural world, some targets fail to acknowledge that planetary boundaries are not negotiable or adaptable to national circumstances or specific situations. Hence, for real transformative change to happen, all SDGs would need a clear-cut commitment to ending and reversing the current trespassing of planetary boundaries. But there are still too many compromises on ecological integrity (Eisenmenger et al. 2020: 1106–1108). Consequently, even if all SDGs were achieved, the world would most likely not be the happy place with humanity living in harmony with nature, nurturing sustainable lifestyles across the globe. And not to forget, there is a contradictory nature between some of the goals and targets, pulling in opposite directions. Hence, managing the trade-off and finding the right compromise between pushing growth and infrastructure on the one hand, and respecting planetary limits and boundaries on the other is making things even more difficult.

When looking at the all-encompassing nature of the 2030 Agenda with the SDG set comprising all aspects of life, one can see the SDGs as the great full-fledged plan for the world or as a too complex and too general compendium, lacking focus, priorities, and real commitment in critical areas. The global nature of the SDGs is both a strength and a weakness. It is a compromise between the desire and the necessity to address everyone everywhere, and at the same time address the concrete challenges, as variegated as they are in conflict and crisis, in the rainforests or in areas shaped by outdated and polluting industries. When the whole world comes together and tries to find common ground about the most urgent challenges and how to ensure a prosperous future for all within planetary boundaries, this inevitably will entail compromise and caveat. And unavoidably and unfortunately, this will produce language ambiguous and vague enough to satisfy all wishes, fears, and desired interpretations.

But beyond all criticism of the SDGs, they also deserve considerable merit and praise for having decisively further developed the sustainability agenda and the range of action for advancing sustainability. A major new aspect was explicitly recognizing the economic dimension of sustainable development and the role of the private sector. Coming from a once rather awkward and uneasy relationship between UN and public action and the private sector, the SDGs are novel and progressive in openly embracing and including the business world as an indispensable partner. However, as overdue and imperative this new partnership was, as unspecific and underdeveloped remains its content. There are many inspiring and trailblazing initiatives by the corporate world and also in cooperation with public actors, for net-zero carbon emissions, zero waste or zero footprint goals. There are likewise numerous financing initiatives for ramping up funding for and investing in sustainability. But these are just coalitions of the willing. And so far, they are rather unlikely to mobilize enough private capital flows or engagement by the private sector in general to substantially advance sustainability or the SDGs fast enough to reach the 2030 deadline.

Another important novel and crucial aspect of the 2030 Agenda was advancing the power of science and the role research and innovation play in achieving sustainability. Evidence based decision-making, undergirded by data and sound measuring, has gained unprecedented attention, fostering ways of quantifying progress or setbacks beyond political interpretation. Hugely important strides have been made in measuring social reality which is an extremely difficult undertaking, anyway. Furthermore, with sustainability science spawning more research on economic and environmental sustainability, it has become very clear that achieving sustainability means to hit the moving target. While science has uncovered and proven the dramatic and long-term impact of, for example, climate change, plastic pollution, or the loss of biodiversity, it has equally revealed that there are still many knowledge gaps about the human impact on the functioning of ecosystems, their capacities and limits. And most importantly, there is much more research needed to identify truly sustainable solutions as the full scale of side effects is often revealing only years later. Thus, unlike fighting poverty, where it would be rather clear to state when this goal was achieved, it appears almost impossible to say when the whole world will have crossed the finish line of having reached a path of sustainable development.

Lessons learned: What the SDGs should and could do for the world

When the 2030 Agenda was adopted in September 2015, there was a huge wave of enthusiasm about the new global goals, a level of excitement that was unimaginable when the process was kickstarted in 2012. Despite all differences, UN member states had managed to come together and agree on this new comprehensive agenda. The momentum to ignite a truly global transformation was palpable. This emotional embracing of the SDGs was also in stark contrast to the wary skepticism when the MDGs were launched 15 years earlier.

But the UN had seen enthusiasm before, and moving from words to action has always been tedious, often producing frustration, missed opportunities, and vitriol. Looking back at previous international agreements reveals a mixed picture but also interesting insights. When in 1992 the Earth Summit adopted the Agenda 21, a sustainable development plan for halting and reversing environmental degradation and pollution, the enthusiasm about this new agenda was ubiquitous and tangible. However, five years later most of this excitement was gone, and during a review meeting at the UN, the room was filled with disappointment and mutual recriminations who or what was responsible for thwarting progress (Dodds et al. 2017: 150; IISD – Earth Negotiations Bulletin 1997). Similarly, the Rio+20 summit in 2012 was largely marked by disillusion and frustration about the failed implementation of the Rio summit decisions 20 years earlier. And delegations were painfully aware that another declaration and another outcome document would hardly be enough to get things moving.

Could this equally happen to the 2030 Agenda? Those who participated in the negotiations and had been living this fascinating time of laying the ground for a sustainable development agenda with drafting the goals and targets are, of course, more confident: "The 2030 Agenda ... will, we hope, have a transformative impact on the lives of billions of human beings, in this and future generations" (Dodds et al. 2017: 129). And yet, with the SDGs in their second halftime, there is an awful feeling of a déjà-vu, a blatant gap between talk and action.

One impressing example how change was successfully initiated and sustained over many years is the Montreal Protocol, a UN treaty signed in 1987. Damaging effects of ozone-depleting substances allowed increased UV rays to reach the earth, leading to growing rates of skin cancer, eye diseases, and noxious effects on the agriculture. The Montreal Protocol was a game-changer as it led to the phase-out of 99 percent of ozone-depleting chemicals in refrigerators, air-conditioners and other consumer products and, thus, helped replenishing the protective ozone layer. At World Ozone Day on September 16, 2019, the UN Environmental Programme (UNEP) proudly announced that this successful international agreement had led to a continuing recovery of the ozone layer, and its complete healing could be predicted for the coming decades.[2]

Could the SDGs draw some inspiration from this success? Most probably only to some limited extent. Saving the ozone layer was a clearly defined, very specific technical issue, boiling down to banning ozone-depleting substances, notably CFCs (chlorofluorocarbons). To resolve it, only some technical innovations were needed without major disruptions in economic processes or consumption behavior. Spraying bottles or refrigerators today simply use different substances but basically didn't change, nor was their very existence ever questioned. Saving the ozone layer was a clearly delineated and easy to understand single issue without major disruptive repercussions.

Another interesting international agreement is the UN Framework Convention on Climate Change (UNFCCC). Agreed in 1992 at the Rio summit, the yearly COP (Conference of the Parties) gatherings were set up three years later as the supreme decision-making body of the climate agenda. Subsequently, they produced crucial milestones, such as the Paris Climate Agreement in 2015. Since then, the climate agenda has turned into the currently largest annual meetings convened by the UN, a yearly global happening, unprecedented in attention, attendance, and resources. The COP meetings have rather unexpectedly become an incredibly powerful tool for messaging and advocacy. They also put an annual pressure on governments, forcing them to take the next steps in their climate commitments (Berkhout 2022). In addition, the annual rotation of hosting the COP gives each host country the chance to leave its own footprints, which has considerable potential to trigger engagement and leadership to produce a good result. This can tremendously benefit the whole process, if there is a skillful and ambitious annual host.

Like the Montreal Protocol about the ozone layer, the climate agenda is a single issue than can easily be boiled down to some clear messages. The 1.5-degree target has turned into the catchy and cogent rallying cry of the climate community that resonates with many people. While the climate agenda is producing headlines and sparking public debate and controversy, the SDGs are lacking this clear messaging and rarely garnering comparable public attention. The five Ps of the SDGs, people, planet, prosperity, peace and partnership, apparently are good and simple advocacy messages. But those buzzwords, as undisputed as they are, remain vague and leave it rather open what exactly to change and achieve. No one would seriously contest working for people, planet, prosperity, peace, and partnerships or claim to work for something very different.

However, despite some sophisticated mechanisms of pledges, voluntary contributions and reviews, the climate agenda has likewise turned out to be frustratingly difficult to implement and is facing controversy and backlashes (Stiell/Guterres 2024). Although climate change is easier to grasp than sustainability in general and garnering considerable support, climate action is equally affecting entire economies as well as people's lives in various aspects. It is very much putting into question business models, treasured daily comforts, and conveniences in developed countries and easy access to cheap energy in developing countries. Subsequently, the COPs are unable to deliver the needed breakthroughs to curb the rapidly mounting climate crisis, and pledges and commitments are rarely fully implemented. Also, there is no effective way to deal with reticent and ignorant actors, blocking and thwarting decisive progress. Frustratingly, it looks increasingly impossible to reach the Paris climate pledge of limiting greenhouse gas emissions to keep global warming below 1.5 degrees Celsius and reach carbon neutrality by 2050. Cogent and clear messaging, without doubt, is a clear asset, but after all no guarantee for getting things done. For both, the climate and the sustainability agenda, there is no scarcity of normative scaffoldings, but there is a huge implementation deficit to deliver at the speed and scale needed for a real transformative shift.

When searching for agreements that were rather successfully implemented, naturally, the MDGs with their sweeping results in the fight against poverty come into mind. Governments, donors, civil society all rallied behind the goals, producing a consensus on development cooperation priorities and building momentum around eradicating poverty. Even though it's impossible to attribute all advances in the fight against poverty to the MDGs, they are seen as the decisive accelerator for achieving tremendous progress in boosting education, health, and saving lives in general. Could the SDGs draw some inspiration from this success? Most probably only to some limited extent. It was a rather simple and clear agenda that was convincing, undisputed and appealing to everyone and largely perceived as producing winners only. And change was supposed to happen in developing countries, alleviating the suffering of people, while seemingly not producing any trade-off or any difficult weighing between conflicting goals. In developed countries, no one needed to leave the comfort zone, and entire economies or lifestyles, apart from trade and supply chains, were never seriously put into question.

For many people it is still hard to fathom what exactly sustainable development entails and, most importantly, which key issues make the big difference. Separating recyclable household waste, using public transport or reducing single-use goods are undoubtedly indispensable parts of the sustainability equation, but certainly lack the scale and scope of the aspired transformation. The SDGs and the incredibly complex and difficult to fathom world of sustainable development are full of wicked challenges, potentially producing trade-offs and a lingering wariness who eventually has to foot the bill. Also, they have a hard time delivering undisputed truly sustainable solutions. And the needed change is of an all-encompassing nature. Daily actions such as consumption patterns, business practices and models, individual and collective behavior as well as mentalities and mindsets, all play a role. Thus, vigorously enforcing sustainability standards bears a significant danger of producing uncertainty, rejection, denial, and feelings of being overwhelmed across all societies. Unsurprisingly, politicians and policy-makers usually opt for gradual approaches to not overburden people and businesses and produce too many uncertainties at the same time. As understandable this strategy is, as much this is delivering too little and too late for the pressing sustainability challenges and most of all for nature that is getting closer to irreversible tipping points.

In the end, considering the magnitude of the envisaged transformation, obviously only bold and visionary leadership and political will by governments can make a difference and has the power to "move the world from commitment to action, and from declaration to delivery", as underscored by the UN Secretary-General (United Nations 2023b: XIII). But so far, there is not enough leadership and steadfast commitment to advance fast enough and comprehensively enough on the sustainability journey. The same holds true for the private sector where thorough transformative change to achieve net-zero and sustainability pledges, and to advance toward a circular economy will happen only through visionary leadership and high-level engagement. But so far, despite many inspiring and dedicated corporate sustainability initiatives, it's not enough to transition at the necessary speed and scale toward sustainable economies.

With a view to what could be effectively done until 2030, it clearly would help the cause to be pragmatic and identify where targeted action would produce the greatest transformative change and boost progress across several goals. During the post-2015 negotiations, all sides were eager to politically treat all issues as equal and, thus, avoid fruitless debates about pitting development against the environment. But, given the urgency to address rising poverty rates and looming ecologically irreversible damage, prioritizing and focusing on what really is game-changing is also a question of credibility of the SDGs. The remaining time for bold and transformative change to achieve tangible results is inexorably and irrevocably running out. If action on rising hunger, runaway climate change, or destruction of ecosystems and biodiversity is failing and not able to prevent deteriorating living conditions all over the world, the whole sustainability agenda faces the danger of being one more piece in the collection of UN agreements that ended up as paper tigers.

The Sustainable Development Solutions Network (SDSN), for example, in 2019 proposed to focus on six key transformations as building blocks: education, health, energy and industry, food and ecosystems, cities and digitalization. All of these would contribute to multiple SDGs, and possible trade-offs with environmental goals would be addressed by adhering to the principles of a circular economy and decoupling (Sachs et al. 2019). The independent scientists, producing the Global Sustainable Development Report, in 2019 proposed and in 2023 reiterated key interventions through six entry-points, identifying them as crucial areas where action could have the biggest impact across the goals: poverty, economies, food systems, energy, urbanization, and the environment. These should be complemented with so-called levers of transformation to galvanize the envisaged change: governance, economy and finance, science and technology, and individual and collective action as well as capacity-building (United Nations 2023b: 103–110). There are other similar proposals about thematic clusters or fundamental transformations (e.g., van Vuuren et al. 2022), where targeted action in specific areas most likely could decisively advance the sustainability agenda and make the biggest difference.

While all these proposals certainly would need an additional fleshing out of specific priorities in different local contexts, they provide a valuable basis for identifying where to concentrate on for using the time until 2030 most effectively. But regardless of possible key areas or priorities where to take action, it is equally important to identify what kind of action would produce the desired results. In 2015, the Addis agreement, providing a plethora of so-called means of implementation, was explicitly drafted to ensure that the SDGs would not just remain on paper but turned into action right from the start. Basically, this was a consequence of the MDG era where the ways and means of fighting poverty were only contrived later over the years. Nevertheless, despite this innovative approach of the Addis Agenda, it was basically listing options. But these hardly ushered in the desired action. Hence, with a view to what is realistic and possible until 2030, it would be essential for governments and other stakeholders to identify effective policies and measures to produce substantial and measurable progress on the SDGs.

However, despite all weaknesses and shortcomings of the SDGs, despite all criticism about them being vastly underfunded, being too lax, too vague, and too numerous, and being subject to whimsical politics, the world has nevertheless tremendously benefitted alone from their very existence.

When the MDGs were launched, they opened up a political space about development and poverty eradication. Through campaigns, political high-level meetings, and civil society advocacy, the poverty agenda was kept on the radars of governments and international organizations, instilling research, debates, and new approaches in the fight against poverty. The politics of global summitry at the UN and other international organizations at times looks like a grand circus, a theater with different stages and performances. But still, it's also an arena for advocacy, political pressure, and creating space for leadership, inspiration, vision, and accountability. The MDGs were far from perfect, but in human and historical terms, they very well served the cause of perfectly framing and tremendously advancing humankind's quest for ending poverty.

The same is true for the SDGs: they have been opening up a political space, spawning visions about a sustainable future, and inspiring and fomenting technological and social disruption, innovation, and invention throughout all aspects of economies and societies. Like the MDGs, the SDGs are far from perfect, but they have been serving as an invaluable compass for the world. They are the guiding light between idealism and realism, between vision and specific every-day challenges. In many ways the SDGs spurred exploring many unbeaten paths, testing new approaches, and fleshing out new forms of partnerships and cooperation models. And much of this is in full swing and likely to generate more traction. The SDGs clearly don't offer enough guidance how to explicitly address specific challenges in specific contexts. In the end, it is left to every government, organization, company, and every single person what to make out of them. But they help crystallize a common understanding of where a change of course is desperately needed and where the world should head to. Through incorporating conflicting aims and wicked sustainability challenges, they also reflect the immense difficulties of carving out the right pathway towards sustainability, and the key role of science in advancing knowledge and identifying truly sustainable solutions.

They very much and very well serve as the constantly ringing alarm bells of the looming catastrophe with business as usual. They are the rallying cries of activists in the lead-up to 2030, keeping up the political, moral, and economic pressure on those who bear responsibilities for enacting change. They are the relentless appeals that everyone can contribute to sustainable lifestyles and economies, and that eradicating poverty and living a decent life is possible for everyone while still preserving a livable environment. The SDGs are uplifting people's minds with heralding the path to a brighter and better future for all humankind. But there is still a long way to go in awareness raising, shifting of mindsets, and prompting a real buy-in. The looming deadline 2030, hopefully, will turn on the heat on governments and all sorts of stakeholders to ramp up targeted action on the global goals. The only thing certain is that business as usual and doing more of the same is by far failing the promise to ignite a sustainable global transformation. Thus, sailing into uncharted waters, venturing out into the open and thinking beyond traditional policies and programs eventually will make or break the SDGs.

Finally, in times of mounting geopolitical divisions and rifts, the SDGs, apart from some exceptions, remain largely uncontested and serve more than ever as a valuable uniting cause and vision, going beyond political fragmentation and polarization. Despite governments coming and going, global crises, including the global COVID-19 pandemic or the recent wars, the convening power of the 2030 Agenda is still very much alive and kicking. The SDGs have proven to be the common ground where the world comes together, a unifying compass about the existential threats for humankind and where humanity has to take action.

Not fulfilling all MDGs at the time was a moral and ethical unbearable failure and not acceptable for the world and humankind. But, as terrible as this might sound, the consequences were largely felt in the developing countries but not threatening humankind in its existence. But failing on the SDGs and going sustainable, however, could mean letting the earth slip into a state with irreversibly degraded ecosystems, depriving much of humankind of a decent life and, in the worst case, eventually turning the earth into a place not inhabitable for humans any more. While the MDGs could still be seen as a choice, although one that would be morally highly reprehensible, sustainability is not a choice any more but a fundamental necessity for the future of humankind (Sanwal 2015: 31–32). Eliminating poverty, enabling decent lives for all, and at the same time not overstepping planetary boundaries is the most complex endeavor that was ever undertaken. But it is an endeavor that is not a "nice to have," it is a "must" without leeway for an overtime or a second try. Failing achieving sustainable living on earth, without doubt, will impact the poor the first and the most, but the consequences will be felt everywhere, no matter if rich or poor, big or small. Sustainable development is a truly global task with no excuse, no escape, and certainly no free lunch and no waiver.

The future is now: Getting ready for post-2030

Until 2030, all efforts should be concentrated on advancing the SDGs as much as possible. Nevertheless, the years before they expire is also the time to draw conclusions from the lessons learned and strategically think ahead. Understanding their strengths and weaknesses is essential when exploring what should and could follow post-2030. And 2027 is the year the HLPF is considering how to advance sustainable development within the UN beyond 2030, as decided in "The Pact for the Future" in September 2024.

Thus, the closing of this book is pondering and discussing some ideas, which will hopefully serve the conversation to generate some inspiration and input for whatever will eventually materialize post-2030. Options, so far, are ranging between simply continuing with the existing SDGs and just extending the deadline until 2050 (e.g., Sachs et al. 2024: 4), updating and tweaking the goals and targets, opening up all goals and targets and negotiating new ones, or drafting a completely new agreement with a new structure. When looking back at the post-2015 process, if this could be the model to emulate for post-2030, this has to be seen in the context of its time: both the Rio process and the MDG process had reached an end and a critical juncture, and the international community was ready to head into a new era. In 2030, the situation most likely will be very different. Most of the topics covered by the SDGs continue being as urgent and decisive for a livable future as when they were debated over a decade ago. Setting out on a path towards sustainable development remains the urgent endeavor of the century all over the world. No one is seriously putting the overarching aims of the 2030 Agenda into question, and no one is advocating for alternative issues being more urgent or more important for a better future.

However, updating the goals and targets, as reasonable as this sounds, means opening up the negotiated agenda and engaging in official UN negotiations. As post-2015 already was a lengthy and incredibly difficult negotiation process, there is the danger of ending up in another even lengthier and more controversial process. And the outcome would be highly uncertain, not necessarily of a higher quality or more focused on the urgent challenges. It looks rather daunting whether renegotiating all goals and targets could produce enough benefit to be worth the effort and the energy that would be consumed by such a process. "The Pact of the Future," eventually adopted in September 2024, already gave some potential foretaste in this regard. It was supposed to mend eroded trust and reiterate commitment to global cooperation in the framework of the 2030 Agenda. As there is general consensus about the importance and relevance of the SDGs, this was assumed to be easy. But it went through months of painful and frustrating negotiations shaped by the current geopolitical divides, and it was unclear until the very last minute, if the pact would garner enough support. In the end, the Summit of the Future only scantly escaped the fate of ending up as a meaningless gathering. Negotiating the Pact of the Future had very much illustrated how divided the world is and how little readiness and willingness there is to join hands and tackle global challenges.

But just extending the deadline to 2050 in view of potentially vitriolic negotiations appears likewise a depressing prospect, equaling a resignation: UN member states shy away from mustering forces for a more effective global commitment that would be about no less than potentially the pathway to saving the world, out of fear of a difficult process. Humankind can't afford riding difficulties out, considering that sustainable transformation is of utmost urgency.

As discussed, some of the targets and respective indicators are of a higher quality than others. Also, as science is advancing, research and development continue broadening and deepening the knowledge about the impact of human action on nature. As going sustainable is an ongoing learning and adapting challenge, it would be extremely useful to incorporate the latest knowledge, in particular better focusing the targets on the essential and ensuring their measurability. If it was possible to do this without getting lost in a political negotiation process for years that could potentially tear the whole sustainable development agenda apart, that would clearly benefit the sustainability journey.

But, even if an updating along the latest scientific knowledge was possible, for instance just updating the targets while leaving the goals untouched, this still wouldn't answer the pertinent question of how to move from words to action, how to achieve the dearly needed transformative change. Updating or even redrafting the goals and targets alone wouldn't necessarily produce more effective action for the neediest, or materialize in the private sector doubling down on its sustainability engagement. Therefore, specific accompanying action plans, apparently are a crucial complement. The Addis Agenda, specifically drafted for facilitating implementing the SDGs, was full of good intentions and ideas but failed to usher in creative and innovative ways of making the SDGs come true. Post-2030 needs to do better, in particular the means of implementation, and to nail down how the specific action would unfold over the years and who would be in the lead for steering the process and the follow-up. In particular, innovative ways of involving and cooperating with the private sector have to be fleshed out. The UN has to go beyond issuing guidelines and recommendations. Notably, it's overdue that UN agencies and multilateral development banks take the next steps in working with the business world. They should have much more room to cooperate with the private sector, to draw in and put to use private funding. Thus, post-2030 can't just be about updating or redrafting the 2030 Agenda and the SDGs, it particularly has to be about redrafting the Addis agreement, the means of implementation, identifying smarter and effective mechanisms for action, and ensuring their sustained achievement, including financing.

Two of the major criticisms of the 2030 Agenda were the broad and general character of the agenda, covering everything under the sun and, thus, losing focus, depth, and understanding what to achieve, and the legally non-binding character which makes the SDGs a good-will exercise. Interestingly, in the aftermath of the 2030 Agenda there are examples that provide valuable insights in how to possibly complement the agenda and, thus, to some extent compensate these deficits.

The goal on climate change rather inadvertently opened up the case how to further differentiate the sustainability agenda. By simple default, the timelines of the post-2015 negotiations and the next COP climate negotiations were crossing their respective paths. The adoption of the 2030 Agenda was scheduled for the UN General Assembly in September 2015, and the adoption of the Paris Agreement for December 2015. Aware of the two negotiations culminating in important agreements with only a few months in between, delegations had been discussing the relationship between the two tracks intensely. On the one hand, each track had its own history and relevance, on the other hand both were dealing with sustainable development and were clearly overlapping to some extent. Strictly separating and ignoring the respective other track would have undermined the credibility of both the climate track and the sustainable development agenda as these were supposed to go hand in hand. Thus, the solution was to formulate a rather general SDG on climate change, leaving all the room and the more specific commitments to the Paris Agreement under the UNFCCC (Caballero/Londoño 2022: 180).

As unimportant as this episode might seem, as interesting is the result of this coincidence, pointing to how to deal with overlapping layers of sustainable development. In the case of climate, the 2030 Agenda eventually ended up providing only the frame for the climate topic that was then further negotiated and fleshed out in detail in another setting, focusing on climate only. There are other specialized agreements, focusing on one specific issue, that followed suit: the Kunming-Montreal Biodiversity Framework in 2022, the resolution about ending plastic pollution in 2022, and the UN Agreement for the Protection of the Ocean or "Treaty of the High Seas" in 2023. Interestingly, the thematic focus of these different agreements also paved the way for making most of them legally binding. The Paris Agreement is a legally binding international treaty that entered into force in November 2016. The resolution on plastic pollution, adopted in March 2022, aims to create an international legally binding instrument on plastic pollution to be concluded in 2025.[3] The Ocean Agreement, adopted in June 2023, provides that those countries that ratify the agreement will be legally bound by it once 60 states have signed and ratified it. By April 2025, already 21 countries had completed those procedures.[4] Only the Biodiversity Agreement is not legally binding.

Specialized and single-topic agreements have a lot of potential to unfold impactful leverage, visibility and traction for their specific issues. Even for the general public, their aim is relatively clear. And in times of increased earmarked funding, it is also easier to establish a dedicated fund and mobilize financing for one specific challenge. Also, they have much better chances of reaching a truly ambitious level, even though they might come with hard-fought battles and sometimes watered-down compromises. But most importantly there is no horse-trading with other issues that don't have anything to do with each other. UN negotiations are usually guided by the overriding precept of "nothing is agreed until everything is agreed." This opens up ample possibilities for any government to block or derail long and complex negotiations because of a globally negligible issue that might be of importance to one or some few actors. During the post-2015 negotiations, there were many nearly dead ends and deadlocks as some delegations were threatening to thwart the entire 2030 Agenda because of some specific wording regarding Common But Differentiated Responsibilities (CBDR), sexual and reproductive health and rights or occupied territories. As important and sensitive these issues are to some countries, they shouldn't be used to take commitments to quality education and health care for poor people, to renewable energies, or to protecting forests and biodiversity hostage. Thematically broad and comprehensive UN negotiations have considerable potential for missing out on key issues and getting lost in a secondary theater of war, or the whole process being bogged down by a single minor concern.

Hence, one option that deserves further discussion, is to have some kind of umbrella agreement, be it a revisited declaration of the 2030 Agenda or some successor agreement, to provide the vision, the course, and the general principles and tenets. This umbrella could be undergirded by headline goals or thematic pillars below, agreed on in respective separate negotiations to specifically avoid this horse-trading. The six entry-points, proposed by the scientists in the Global Sustainable Development Report, for example, or the six key areas, proposed by the SDSN, are valuable thematic pools from which to draw ideas for potential future headline goals or thematic pillars (see also Cernev/Fenner 2024, who propose seven goals), undergirding a general and common frame. While the MDGs and the SDGs both had a 15-year implementation time, for post-2030 often the year 2050 comes up as the potential next deadline. This would facilitate the needed long-term planning, with some interim milestones to be reached in-between, but also very well align with the Paris climate goal of achieving carbon neutrality by 2050. Thus, from an advocacy point of view, 2050 could be the time horizon and rallying cry for a comprehensive sustainability agenda, calling for reaching net-zero carbon and net-zero material footprint in line with a circular economy over a 20-year implementation period.

So far, when it comes to learning from the SDGs, most conclusions underscore one point: post-2030 should be leaner, clearer, and more focused on what is game-changing. Many deliberations are in favor of simplifying and reducing the sustainability agenda and largely boil down to three overarching areas: eradicating poverty and enabling all people to live in dignity, transforming all activities into circular economy models with net-zero emissions and a net-zero material footprint, and preserving planetary health and accepting planetary boundaries as the frontier, confining and limiting all human activity. These reflect the three dimensions of sustainable development, pinpointing to and delineating clearly what to achieve.

Subsequently, further complementing possible headline goals or thematic pillars with strategies, action plans, and dedicated funding, and possibly also adding legally binding agreements on specific topics, where possible, definitely deserves further consideration. Designing different layers of responsibility and detail, comes with significant advantages of burden-sharing. A framework agenda would be upholding the shared vision, values, and principles, highlighting the interlinkages and interdependencies between all topics but without getting lost in the nitty-gritty details. Respective complementary headline goals or thematic pillars below could be spelling out the substance of the needed action, whom to involve and what to achieve, notably including how to ensure the financing. Furthermore, consistently applying science-based criteria when defining goals, targets, and indicators would be essential for ensuring that progress is tracked in a sound and comprehensive way.

Adding legally binding agreements on specific issues, where possible and useful, would be a valuable complement to such a framework. The already existing agreements on climate change, biodiversity, plastic pollution, or oceans, currently complementing some single SDGs, are very much going in this direction. But, while there are easy to define and delineate challenges with specific actors to be involved that can be very well covered by a single agreement, there are other issues that are far more complex. For example, transitioning towards a circular economy is a much more comprehensive undertaking than eliminating plastics or protecting the oceans. Also, it is hard to see how eradicating poverty, which is a crucial part of the 2030 Agenda and has to be a fundamental commitment of any post-2030 agreement, could be meaningfully covered by a legally binding agreement. Hence, having complementary single-issue agreements has considerable potential to accelerate targeted action on some specific topics to mobilize awareness, resources, political leverage and impact. But it looks unlikely that these could accelerate all SDGs or their successors and meaningfully cover all important issues.

However, that said, legally binding agreements, as powerful as they look, are not the magic formula for getting things done. The Paris Climate

Agreement, once being praised as a landmark agreement that caters to the respective country situation through the flexibility of self-determined pledges to reduce emissions, is equally in deep trouble. Many commitments made by governments are still not being implemented. The countries are legally bound to submit their national pledges every five years, but they are not obligated to comply with them. The Paris Agreement even set up an Implementation and Compliance Committee that works in a supportive and facilitative way, but it doesn't resolve any conflicts nor imposes any penalties or sanctions. There is no further enforcement mechanism; subsequently, it's impossible to enforce compliance. Political and social pressure on government policies and behavior remains the most important tool. Many countries have made net-zero pledges by 2050 or 2060, seemingly responding to their international obligations and the pressure, but there is considerable doubt, if these are feasible and realistic. For international agreements, thus, functional and smart mechanisms are urgently needed that enhance compliance and ensure accountability in an effective way. There are valuable lessons learned from the Paris Agreement about what propels compliance (see, e.g., Stankovic et al. 2023; Van Lierop 2019), but there is no ideal solution yet, in particular for complex long-term agreements. So far, an international enforcement body for international agreements or some overarching judicial compulsory system to address non-compliance don't exist and most probably never will be set up. Usually, governments deem this as a meddling into their national sovereignty.

Hence, regarding the 2030 Agenda or a successor agenda, making such a comprehensive and all-encompassing agreement legally binding, appears neither feasible nor desirable. The outcome could only be a rather watered-down document, leaving enough room for interpretation for everyone to agree. Thus, for post-2030, it's rather unlikely that there would be appetite to strive for a legally binding agenda. However, what could provide critical impetus is applying consistent risk assessments, depicting what it possibly entails to miss out on certain results. As there are many thresholds and natural boundaries that should be avoided crossing, having a common analysis of the probability and the potential consequences could significantly help turning global risk assessments into policy tools. These could be guiding mitigation and accelerated risk-aware action to prevent projected famine, soil degradation or polluted rivers, depleted natural resources or malfunctioning ecosystems, economic downturns or natural disasters. Attaching a price-tag on action versus inaction could facilitate targeted engagement towards at least preventing the worst to happen.

For whatever succeeds in 2030, addressing the most glaring deficiencies and urgent sustainability challenges has to be the primary aim.

And discussions should be guided by the prospect of achieving results. Hence, any post-2030 commitment has to produce actionable, measurable steps with enhanced accountability. And most importantly, these have to include not only governments but all essential actors, in particular the private sector, as a key player. This requires a smart policy mix of pressure through regulation and taxation as well as incentives to move toward sustainable business models and economies. But the long-term vision and direction need to be unequivocally clear, and meaningful follow-up procedures and enforcement mechanisms need to be in place to make the global transformation happen.

Finally, the UN despite all its flaws, remains an indispensable forum and the only place where any post-2030 agreement could be born. After all, the UN is still the only place to convene the world to find solutions that are of global concern and are impossible to resolve by groups of nations, let alone by single countries. The world needs a universal body in which all sovereign nations can come together, debate, seek common ground, and devise collective solutions to problems that affect all people. But the UN is struggling to live up to this challenge and risks becoming part of the problems themselves. Thus, enhancing and fostering the UN's ability and capacity to deliver on these tasks and produce the added-value that no single country could produce on its own is essential for serving the sustainability cause. In the end, providing the right frame, the right guidance, and the right mechanisms through the UN bestows an unrivaled and indispensable legitimacy on common global action and can tremendously empower actors to rise up to the challenge and do the seemingly impossible.

In hindsight, the years of the post-2015 process were rather auspicious and favorable times, a window of opportunity for the world to come together and agree on a joint vision for people and the planet. Countries were ready and willing to learn and understand about the challenges humankind all over the world was facing and agreeing on what should be done about them. The 2030 Agenda is a testament to what was politically possible in 2015, an unparalleled feat and the most comprehensive and complete agenda for the world ever adopted. During the post-2015 process, "[t]he stars are aligned for the world to take historic action to transform lives and protect the planet," so the UN Secretary-General (United Nations 2014: 6). Naturally, the stars will be different in 2030, as will be the world, and, for better or worse, eventually produce an agenda, that will be possible in 2030 world politics. Whatever a post-2030 agenda looks like and whatever the further way ahead on the path to sustainability looks like, it will be more than ever critical for people and planet because going sustainable is here to stay as a question of survival for humankind.

Notes

1 By 2024, only three countries have never submitted a VNR: Haiti, Myanmar, and the United States.
2 UNEP press release: "32 Years and Healing", September 16, 2019.
3 https://www.unep.org/news-and-stories/press-release/plastic-pollution-negotiations-adjourn-new-text-and-follow-session
4 https://highseasalliance.org/treaty-ratification/

References

Beisheim, Marianne (2023): Politics Matters! Expert Assessments of the SDG's Political Significance in Selected Countries, in: Marianne Beisheim (Ed.): *Country-Level Politics around the SDGs. Analysing Political Will as a Critical Element of the Mid-Term Review of the 2030 Agenda and the SDGs*, German Institute for International and Security Affairs, SWP Research Paper 7, July 2023, Berlin.

Berkhout, Frans (2022): Climate COP27: Do Climate Summits Make a Difference? King's College London. https://www.kcl.ac.uk/climate-cop27-do-climate-summits-make-a-difference

Biermann, Frank/Thomas Hickmann/Carole-Anne Sénit et al. (2022): Scientific Evidence on the Political Impact of the Sustainable Development Goals. *Nature Sustainability,* Vol. 5, pp. 795–800. https://doi.org/10.1038/s41893-022-00909-5

Bonnedahl, Karl Johan/Pasi Heikkurinen/Jouni Paavola (2022): Strongly Sustainable Development Goals: Overcoming Distances Constraining Responsible Action. *Environmental Science and Policy*, Vol. 129, pp. 150–158.

Caballero, Paula/Patti Londoño (2022): *Redefining Development. The Extraordinary Genesis of the Sustainable Development Goals*, Boulder/London: Lynne Rienner Publishers.

Cernev, Tom/Richard Fenner (2024): Beyond 2030: Structures for Achieving Sustainable Development. *Frontiers in Climate*, October 16, 2024.

Dodds, Felix/David Donoghue/Jimena Leiva Roesch (2017): *Negotiating the Sustainable Development Goals, a Transformational Agenda for an Insecure World,* Oxon/New York: Routledge.

Donoghue, David (2020): Die Verhandlungen zur Agenda 2030 für nachhaltige Entwicklung, in: Vereinte Nationen, 5/2020. The Negotiations on the Agenda 2030 for Sustainable Development.

Eisenmenger, Nina/Melanie Pichler/Nora Krenmayr/Dominik Noll/Barbara Plank/Ekaterina Schalmann/Marie-Theres Wandl/Simone Gingrich (2020): The Sustainable Development Goals Prioritize Economic Growth over Sustainable Resource Use: A Critical Reflection on the SDGs from a Socio-ecological Perspective. *Sustainability Science*, Vol. 15, pp. 1101–1110.

Fukuda-Parr, Sakiko/Natalya Volchkova/Rolph van der Hoeven/Trudi Hartzenberg/Sofia Borges/Ahmed Galal/Xufeng Zhu (2023): *Implementing the SDGs: Strengthening the Voluntary National Reviews (VNRs)*, CDP Background Paper No. 56, ST/ESA/2023/CDP/56.

Hestad, Dina (2021): The Evolution of Private Sector Action in Sustainable Development, in: International Institute for Sustainable Development (ISSD), Earth Negotiations Bulletin Brief #12.

IISD – Earth Negotiations Bulletin (1997): Summary Report, June 23–27, 1997.

Kharas, Homi/John W. McArthur (2024): How Is the World Really Doing on the SDGs? Brookings, November 25, 2024. https://www.brookings.edu/articles/how-is-the-world-really-doing-on-the-sdgs/

Sachs, Jeffrey/Guido Schmidt-Traub/Mariana Mazzucato/Dirk Messner/Nebojsa Nakicenovic/Johan Rockström (2019): Six Transformations to Achieve the Sustainable Development Goals. *Nature Sustainability*, Vol. 2, pp. 805–814.

Sachs, Jeffrey/Guillaume Lafortune/Grayson Fuller (2024): The SDGs and the UN Summit of the Future. Sustainable Development Report 2024, New York, London, Paris. https://doi.org/10.25546/108572

Sanwal, Mukul (2015): *The World's Search for Sustainable Development, a Perspective from the Global South*, Cambridge: Cambridge University Press.

Stankovic, Tatjana/Jon Hovi/Tora Skodvin (2023): The Paris Agreement's Inherent Tension Between Ambition and Compliance. *Humanities & Social Sciences Communications*, Vol. 10, 550. https://doi.org/10.1057/s41599-023-02054-6

Stiell, Simon/António Guterres (2024): Open Letter on COP Reform to All States That Are Parties to the Convention, Executive Secretary of the UNFCCC Secretariat and UN Secretary-General. *The Club of Rome*, November 15, 2024. https://www.clubofrome.org/cop-reform-2024/

UNDESA (2022): Repository of Good Practices in Voluntary National Review (VNR) Reporting, New York.

United Nations (2014): The Road to Dignity by 2030: Ending Poverty, Transforming All Lives and Protecting the Planet. Synthesis report of the Secretary-General on the post-2015 sustainable development agenda, A/69/700, December 4, 2014.

United Nations (2019): The Sustainable Development Goals Report 2019, New York.

United Nations (2021): The Sustainable Development Goals Report 2021, New York.

United Nations (2023a): The Sustainable Development Goals Report 2023, New York.

United Nations (2023b): Global Sustainable Development Report 2023: Times of Crisis, Times of Change: Science for Accelerating Transformations for Sustainable Development, New York.

United Nations (2024): The Sustainable Development Goals Report 2024. New York.

Van Lierop, Wal (2019): The Paris Agreement Needs Teeth, *Forbes*, July 25, 2019.

van Vuuren, Detlef P./Caroline Zimm/Sebastian Busch/Armin von Schiller/Jörn O. Schmidt/Bjoern Soergel (2022): Defining a Sustainable Development Target Space for 2030 and 2050. *One Earth*, Vol. 5, No. 2, pp. 142–156.

World Bank (2024b): Poverty, Prosperity, and Planet Report 2024: Pathways Out of the Polycrisis, Washington DC.

INDEX

FSC
www.fsc.org
MIX
Papier | Fördert
gute Waldnutzung
FSC® C083411

Kolibri 360 GmbH
Ferdinand-Jühlke-Straße 7
99095 Erfurt, Deutschland
produktsicherheit@kolibri360.de